ADAM TORR

PRESENTS

VOLUME 4

BUSINESS LEADERS
EDITION

MISSION
MATTERS

World's Leading Entrepreneurs Reveal their
TOP TIPS TO SUCCESS

FEATURED AUTHORS:

Dr. Alejandro Badia	Kurt Snyder
Ashu Bhatia	La'Shion Robinson
Brian Patrick	Martin Rowinski
Bruce Elfenbein	Michael Ralby
Chris Reavis	Robert Wolf
Eric Aguilar	Sarah Miller
Gregory Shepard	Shannon Wilkinson
J.C. Granger	Stephen Deason
Dr. Joseph McGinley	Dr. Troy Hall

CENTURY CITY

Century City, CA

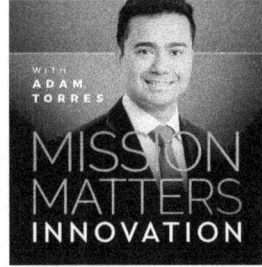

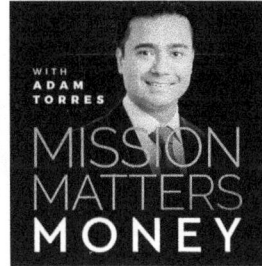

For information, visit **www.MissionMatters.com**

Managing Editor:
Jyssica Schwartz

Graphic Design:
Kendra Cagle

Century City, CA 90067
www.MissionMatters.com

MISSION
MATTERS
WE AMPLIFY STORIES

CENTURY
CITY

The Mr. Century City Logo is a trademark of Mr. Century City, LLC.

ISBN 13: 978-1-949680-35-5

Mission Matters, Beverly Hills, CA

DEDICATION

To the leaders who pay it forward.

TABLE OF CONTENTS

ACKNOWLEDGMENTS

Chirag Sagar, Co-Founder of Mission Matters

Trent Lindsey, Podcast Producer, Mission Matters

The Sagar Family

Jyssica Schwartz, Managing Editor

Christopher Kai, The Mathem Group

Jennifer Y. Chen, President & CEO of HBCS, Inc.

Dan Bienenfeld, President, KERV Interactive

Stella Song, CEO, Digital Luxury Agency

Eric Rosado, CEO, Karma Snack

Michael Douglas Carlin, Editor, Century City News

Dr. Ben Shamoiel, Chiropractor and Founder, The LA Chiropractor

Antonio De Shawn Spears, COO, City Global

Kendra Cagle, 5 Lakes Design

Keyan Razi, Founder & CEO, Impactnext

Patrick Reynoso, Chief Creative Officer, Digital Luxury Agency

Alice Yi, General Counsel, Digital Luxury Agency

Jovana Rizzo, Vice President, BerlinRosen

INTRODUCTION

By **ADAM TORRES**

What does it mean to build a community? The word community has a different meaning and level of seriousness depending on who you ask. For some, a community is where you grew up. You may have a close connection with it and the people, or maybe not so much. For others, their sense of community is deeply rooted in their value system and the way they view the world. This question of community is one that Chirag Sagar (the other co-founder of Mission Matters) and I discuss often.

When we began the Mission Matters brand, we weren't exactly sure if it would catch on. Like all business owners, it was/is our baby, so we want it to grow and be strong and successful. But that is not always the case. Businesses fail for many reasons. We won't go into that here. Instead, I'd like to go further down the path of community. Because I think that is our "secret sauce." For the business owners, entrepreneurs, and professionals reading this, I'd like to pick on myself for a moment. In the beginning, I didn't really understand the importance of community.

Chirag was the advocate of community from the beginning. I can be, at times, slow to change. I blame this on being a Taurus, but that's another story and probably a crutch. As time went on, Chirag worked on me, as many great business partners do, and slowly won me over to his side of things. I thought we were building, selling, and delivering a product. But over time, I realized Chirag was right and that we have the power to change lives.

iii

I think this opportunity exists in all businesses. In fact, I've seen the proof. As I write this, we have released almost 3,000 interviews across the eight podcasts I host. While I don't claim to be an expert in business, every day I learn from the guests I interview. There is often a common trait to the most successful business owners, the ones who really create something unique; it is community. Some businesses may use a different word for this. Maybe brand loyalty? We have all heard that one. But the next step above loyalty is to make the audience/consumer feel like they are part of the brand.

To do this, some companies are really active and personal on social media. Maybe the CEO is really active on Twitter. Other brands do it through amazing customer service. For example, say what you will, but I "feel" like I'm part of the Amazon family. I've been a prime member since it started and take pride in outdoing my orders from the previous year. Last year I placed 143 orders on Amazon. This year my goal is 200. And no, my uncle Jeff Bezos is not paying me to say this. But if he reads this, I'm just appreciative that he created Amazon's print-on-demand service that allows publishers like us to stay in business and grow.

As you read this, you are probably thinking about a brand or two that you have a similar connection to. If you aren't, take a second and think about it. What brand would you speak highly of and continue to support just because they have made you feel so much a part of their community through the years? Your next mission is to think about how you can build a stronger sense of community in whatever line of work you are currently pursuing. The fact that you are trying and making a conscious effort to build a community helps it become self-fulfilling. It will also spill over to other facets of your life and possibly even enhance your personal relationships. Again, I'm not claiming to be an expert on this, I'm just telling you what has happened in my life, both personally and professionally due to this new outlook that Chirag so diligently brainwashed me with over the last 3-4 years.

But the conversation doesn't stop here. We are constantly looking for ways to give back to our community and find new ways to engage in meaningful dialogues. For example, this year we launched our Mission Matters Community Facebook group. It's a place for our podcast guests, readers, and others interested in the community to interact and share tips. We also launched a Mission Matters Virtual Summit series, where I do in-depth interviews spanning many topics. How did we get these ideas? By listening to our community.

This brings me to the book you are holding. I am so proud to welcome this group of 18 new authors into the Mission Matters author community. The authors featured in this book are all from different backgrounds and stages in life. There is one common thread that unites them all: The willingness to share their stories and insights for the benefit of others. It's not an easy thing to make your story public. But the real benefit is adding to the collective knowledge so that current and future generations can benefit.

To your success,

Adam Torres

P.S. Join our community on Facebook at
www.facebook.com/groups/missionmatters

CHAPTER 1

WHERE PATIENT CARE & TECHNOLOGY MEET

By DR. ALEJANDRO BADIA

There are many flaws in the American healthcare system, and unfortunately, many of them are being brought to light now during the COVID-19 pandemic. We can all agree there are glaring holes, but many doctors are working toward more inclusive, efficient, and less invasive options where patients get the care they need without having to spend months or even years being bounced from one place to another.

A perfect example of this is a patient of mine, let's call her Anna. Anna is a waitress at a sports bar in Miami and she suffered a shoulder injury at work when she slipped and fell. Her workman's compensation mandated that she go to an occupational health center. The occupational health center was staffed, as most of them are, by a general family practitioner.

Even though 93% of workman's comp injuries are musculoskeletal, the general practitioners at occupational health centers around the U.S. are not specialized in that area at all. Knowing that the overwhelming majority of work injuries are musculoskeletal, I propose it would make a lot more sense to send the patients to a physician or clinician specialized in those types of injuries. After all, if you have an eye injury, you go directly to an eye doctor, right? You wouldn't start with a general practitioner and then later see an eye doctor.

Because the doctor at the occupational health center is more generalized, they often don't dig too much further, and when they do order additional testing, the patient is referred to another location, sometimes miles away on another day, for MRIs, x-rays, or other tests. Each time another test is run, the patient then has to come back to the health center to get their results - yet another day and another appointment. Those results are usually just the general practitioner reading the report but the patient doesn't know if any of these doctors are experts in her type of injury. These patients are being run around and taking a lot of time and not getting optimal care.

Most often, the physician at the health center orders physical therapy for these types of injuries. Unfortunately, physical therapy can actually exacerbate certain musculoskeletal injuries, not heal them. Anna was sent to physical therapy, where they manipulated and moved her shoulder every week when a clear diagnosis had not yet been made. Furthermore, the person ordering the test may not realize that certain clinical issues may not appear in that diagnostic study and further intervention may be necessary.

Anna spent a year being sent for one test after another and going through physical therapy, but her shoulder was not getting better. She finally requested to be sent to a specialist. When she came to my hand/upper limb office, I was able to do a quick MRI on-site at my location and see that she had a significant rotator cuff tear in her shoulder. We were able to perform surgery at the same location and repair it with shoulder arthroscopy. However, during arthroscopy, we also found a massive labral tear as well (SLAP type 2), which likely explained the ongoing pain and is a much more challenging diagnosis to make in many imaging studies. It was not until the arthroscopic procedure was performed that we could make the definitive diagnosis and is something that should have been done much earlier. Moreover, when patients have ongoing persistent pain despite ample conservative treatment, appropriate intervention is needed since no diagnostic study will actually resolve pain and too much emphasis on "tests" is placed by the non-specialized clinician. Understanding when to intervene requires a clinical gestalt that the orthopedic specialist possesses and has an inherent economic, as well as humane, value.

Labral tears are a fairly common issue but because the general practitioner at the health center didn't know much about it or to look for it, it went undiagnosed while Anna was paying missing work and her workmen's comp insurance company was paying for physical therapy she didn't need for a year. This concept completely eludes the employer who is now out one of their best employees, often having to train someone else to cover.

Anna had to request to see a specialist through the insurance, who told her no several times and tried to push her to keep going to the therapy center. The major irony is that even after surgery, the insurance company tried to control a process they truly don't understand. In Anna's case, they referred her to a therapist unknown to me within 72 hours of surgery, where they began manipulating her shoulder despite the repair I performed. This was because there is NO communication between these clinicians since the bureaucrats control the process, not the caregivers. When the tearful patient presented to my office relating her ordeal, I requested an immediate MRI to ensure that my labral repair was not disrupted, since the manipulative therapy was completely contraindicated. A further irony was that this request was denied despite the machine being literally 20 feet away from the patient's exam room.

The insurance company naturally wants the easiest possible solution but they obviously do not understand how to achieve that since they place barriers and add unnecessary steps to the process. They typically add another filter and another expense to the patient care journey. They thought they were saving money by not doing an "unnecessary" test, despite my office explaining it was necessary.

Anna and her husband chose to simply pay for the MRI outright. Unfortunately, this happens too often in our healthcare system. The insurance company person is not a trained physician, they should not have the authority to say that a doctor-requested test is not necessary.

If Anna's employer, the insurance company, or the health center had simply sent her to see a specialist right away, Anna would have saved a lot of time, money, and pain. One solution would be to use an orthopedic walk-in facility, such as OrthoNOW, where an orthopedic clinician could best decide which test to order, if any, and when to expedite referral to a surgeon, often on the same day when clinically expedient.

Unfortunately, I see this in my own specialty practice every single day. Patients are bounced from one place to another and not getting the care they need in a timely manner. The insurance company is spending more money, the patient is spending more, the patient's employer and family are being impacted, and the care is suffering.

By utilizing technology, my disruptive care company, OrthoNOW, has even devised a tool to allow a general practitioner to have a specialist review x-rays and MRI results to determine if there is a problem. The patient may not even need to see the specialist themselves or be referred to another doctor.

Technology to Enhance Patient Care

Utilizing new technology can address patient care issues and save the healthcare system a lot of money and time.

Due to the COVID-19 pandemic, many physicians are being forced to close their offices or even shut down their practices altogether. Long before this global pandemic, I have used technology to do "telehealth," the practice of virtual appointments. Telehealth allows me to do some examinations, meet with patients, answer questions, explain diagnostics and test results, make a treatment plan, and decide if patients need additional testing or x-rays. Being able to continue working with patients at this time has been invaluable.

Before this crisis, I'd been using telehealth/teleorthopedics for over five years to connect with international patients, do follow-up appointments, and give test results among other things, and telerehab to monitor patients' physical therapy. All of which meant fewer in-person visits and co-pays for the patients and less time they had to take off work to come into the office and fewer claims for the insurance companies. It also saves me time. Everyone involved benefits from the use of technology in healthcare.

While many physicians and practices have resisted using these technologies, I firmly believe that things like telehealth are going to be used far more moving forward due to doctors seeing how extremely useful it is. We may have been forced to adapt in the wake of the pandemic, but these technologies will continue to be useful - even vital - after the pandemic has passed.

Another technology I have been using in my practice is an app designed by a sports medicine specialist in order to expedite care and communication between coaches, trainers, and clinicians. We have three different OrthoNOW locations and SirenMD is a workplace collaboration platform designed to increase the quality, efficiency, and timeliness of medical decisions by facilitating coordinated communication between caregivers and patient care coordinators such as surgical schedulers or therapy center staff.

This app allows clinicians at the OrthoNOW walk-in center to send x-rays or other test results to the appropriate subspecialist from any location to review remotely. The specialist is then able to view studies and consult with the attending doctor to give diagnoses, discuss the right care for the patient, and schedule additional appointments, or even a procedure, in real-time. It basically allows a clinician or non-specialist physician to text and consult with a specialist right away, even from across the world. The app also aggregates injury data and can look for patterns in types of injuries. It's a centralized platform and HIPAA secure and allows easier coordination between doctors of all specialties - so why aren't more practices employing this technology?

An application we developed on our own is our award-winning OrthoNOW app. Referring entities and even patients can easily have the free app on their phone to gain direct access to the nearest OrthoNOW center. This can be of great value to the employer, the insurance carrier, the nonspecialist, and even the patient in pain themselves. Users click on the location and can immediately make an appointment to let the office know they're coming, and explain the injury or upload photos of the injury so the office is set up with whatever the patient will need, such as an x-ray machine ready to go for a wrist injury by the time the patient arrives. Another feature of the OrthoNOW app is the On My Way NOW function, where the app can even call an Uber for the patient to get them to the doctor's office as soon as possible. This app has changed the way we prepare and the rate at which we can care for injuries.

Unfortunately, many healthcare centers and employers are still resistant to implementing the new apps and technology which can make their jobs easier, expedite referrals, and correctly diagnose patients faster.

All of this technology already exists and can make the entire process for both patients and physicians less stressful, less expensive, and more efficient. But many doctors and insurance companies still resist it and most patients don't know it even exists. The average person often assumes "doctor tech" is just making an appointment online or getting texts that their prescription is ready.

Other Ways Physicians Can Employ Technology

It's not just apps, either. Technology within healthcare has been advancing rapidly over the last couple of decades. X-ray machines, ultrasounds, and MRIs have been used for many years, but they are all continuously being advanced in fascinating ways.

At my practice, we now use augmented reality in conjunction with ultrasounds to see the ultrasound image superimposed directly onto a patient. This is helpful in many ways, one being that as the doctor performs a procedure, such as PRP injections, I don't have to turn away from the patient to look at the ultrasound screen while placing and making an injection, which saves time and can save the patient from extra pain of the procedure taking longer.

Instead, I have a pair of goggles that project the live ultrasound image directly on the patient's skin. It's not virtual reality, I am not in a computer-generated simulation, it is computer-generated content overlaid on real-world environments. I am able to see through the goggles like a pair of glasses and see the image directly on top of the patient.

Augmented reality has been available to doctors since the 1960s and has continued to get better and find more uses with time. It can be used in surgeries to get a better, more accurate view of what is happening with the patient, it's used in neurosurgery, and even to find veins more easily to draw blood or put in an IV.

We also employ fluoroscopy, a live study of moving body structures similar to seeing x-rays as a moving image. It helps in both diagnosing injuries and also has surgical applications. For example, I can do live fluoroscopy to see if there is carpal instability or look at fractures without needing a CT scan or MRI. In fact, since using fluoroscopy, I rarely ever order CT scans anymore. Another example of fluoroscopy being used is in cardiology, where a doctor can use it to see the flow of blood through the arteries and evaluate if there are any blockages.

Fluoroscopy can also be used to locate foreign things in the body, do image-guided injections into a patient's joints or spine with more precision, and treat compression fractures in the spine. In addition, fluoroscopy machines are regulated by the Food and Drug Administration (FDA) and are considered safe and effective.

It's Time To Change How We Use Technology in the Medical Field

The technology I discussed in this chapter is all available and being used in many industries already. It is crazy to think that in an industry as important as healthcare, many old-school ideas and behaviors and technologies are still being employed.

Technology has the ability to speed up how quickly we can correctly diagnose a patient, change the way patients interact with doctors, and save everyone both time and money.

Why isn't it everywhere? Well, in the American healthcare system, a lot of people not in direct patient care make too much money to want to institute a lot of changes. Insurance companies make money from sometimes-unnecessary testing and office visits and medications. They are the middlemen to every doctor-patient interaction. They also control the money, being able to request or deny procedures, despite not knowing what is best for the patient. It's not the researchers developing new medications or the doctors who benefit most or make the most money in any of these situations, it's the insurance companies.

But as medical technology advances and more physicians are experimenting and becoming more efficient, things are trending in the right direction. I may have some ideas for how we can keep up with other industries and I've spoken with and interviewed other professionals to write a book about what real day-to-day healthcare looks like and what it could be in the future expanding on the information in this chapter. *Healthcare From the Trenches* was released on June 15, 2020, and you can purchase it now on Amazon.

CHAPTER 2

DIGITAL LEADERSHIP IN THE NEW WORLD

By **ASHU BHATIA**

The WHY and WHY NOW - Digital Imperative

As one reads about the pandemic and as many industries are grappling with digitization, the term "Digital Transformation" is even more omnipresent - it has become imperative. One of my clients said it best, "When the doctor told you over the years that exercise and diet are good for your heart, you listened and thought 'I'll get to it soon.' When he says that you might have a heart attack next week, you are on with the regimen that afternoon." That's how the digital acceleration feels amidst this pandemic. It's a mandate and hyper-prioritization for both the top line and bottom line is key. The impact on supply chains and workplace transformation is being addressed feverishly. It makes one wonder WHY is this so relevant and WHY NOW suddenly.

It boils down to three main trends:
- **Speed** - Disruption of business models through technology has been around for quite some time, but what is different this time is the pace of change and the adoption of new technology at hyperspeed. The impact is evident by looking at the growth curve of consumer engagement to reach 50 million users: Radio – 38 years; TV – 13 years; Internet – 4 years; Facebook – 8 months; Pokemon Go – a few hours.

- **Sweep** – The power of these technologies is truly global, with platforms stitching together apps for worldwide consumers. As an analogy to the physical world, there was a time when Coca-Cola products were only for the elite. Now pretty much everyone on the planet knows and uses their products. In a very similar manner, people in all economies - developed, developing, and emerging - are adopting digital technologies.

- **Scope** - Since digital technologies are invading most industries and across the value chains, there is the concept of Digital Ecosystems. One company that is a great case study is the Chinese firm Tencent with its messaging application, WeChat. Initially a messaging app, it has evolved into a lifestyle platform with 850 million monthly active users. It is now a platform that allows users to share things on social media, order food, book doctors' appointments, receive coupons, and now even conduct financial transactions. The way to look at it is this: Your smartphone is not just a phone - it is an entertainment tool, a calculator, your credit card, a computer, etc. There is an almost fusion happening within and outside of the established ecosystems to establish such 'super apps' to propel businesses forward.

These combined forces are changing the *way value is **delivered** and **consumed***. Thinking of two dimensions is key to put a reference on your existing digital acceleration journey: Customer Experience (CX) and Employee Experience (EX).

1. **An External Focus** - Customer Experience (CX) is key to meeting higher customer expectations, having consistency across touchpoints, and becoming less siloed in systems and

culture. Companies always focused on CX in varied capac-
ities. But it was usually the unplanned result of customers
interacting with the different parts of a company. A better
approach is starting from the outside-in - defining the desired
customer experience and organizing your business to deliver
it. Just like the Six Sigma methodology of Voice of Customer
(VOC), the software designers realized that understanding
every customer touchpoint and the experience behind each
will make better products.

    a.   For example, in the hospitality industry, everything
starts with an idea, search, pre-transaction, in-tran-
sit, and post-transaction (awareness, usage, and
experience residual). True digital leaders look at the
customer experience at each touchpoint and also
focus on workforce transformation at each of those
points to truly affect change.

2. **An Internal Focus** – Employee experience (EX) truly leads
to the needed customer experience. Digital transformation
requires more than automation but the ease of use to insti-
tutionalize the capabilities so employees can offer that to the
final consumers. Some examples of this are as below:

    a.   Delivering an *intelligent back-office* - accelerating
employee decisions through analytics leads to cost
reduction and superior service simultaneously.

    b.   Enabling the *connected workforce* – employees are so
distributed these days across geographies and time
zones with no real-time connection to management,

especially in a post-COVID world. Connecting them through the collaboration processes and tools is key to empower the workforce.

c. Deliver the *next-generation* colleague experience – as younger generations enter the workforce, you have to ensure that their experience from recruitment to retirement is designed for and delivering on their expectations.

Clearly all customer touchpoints are dictated by only one word– EXPERIENCE. That is what the process and technology platforms have to deliver and enable the human or system to interact with the customer.

The WHAT - Levers for change

At its simplest level, digital transformation is about using digital technology to change the way we do business. As simple as that sounds, it represents sweeping changes across every industry. Just like a car runs on many gears, digital transformation is enabled only by the appropriate use of all technologies as necessary. The industry is abuzz with technology being leveraged to offer this - SMACIT (social, mobile, analytics, cloud, and Internet of Things).

It is important to look at these and have a holistic strategy around each of the ingredients in your digital recipe. It's the confluence of these technologies that truly creates a unique competitive advantage. Some companies undertake this transformation in a piecemeal fashion and struggle to know where to start.

Cloud Computing

For anyone reading the technology evolution, the Journey-to-Cloud is a mandate to understand. The technology evolution from mainframe to client-server and now to the cloud and edge computing is intriguing. Cloud-based computing and storage platforms offer many advantages over conventional on-premise systems, from lower operating costs to better compatibility with the working styles of digital enterprises. If your destination is a modern customer experience, then cloud is the highway: Elasticity of demand, OpEx matching revenue for experimentation in front-end systems, and newer operating models are the lanes on this road.

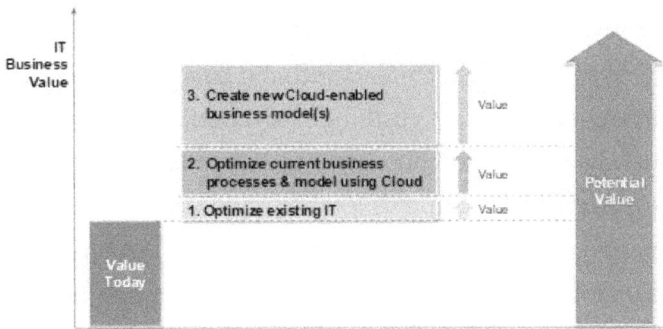

Artificial Intelligence (AI)

Almost every business and technology professional recognizes the importance of data and analytics but struggles with how to operationalize AI initiatives to generate business impact from these data insights. This concern has its roots in the need for a 'mindset.' It's about skill and simple usage of these insights that are at the core of the issue. Leadership needs to embrace this and prepare the workforce for the digital future by reskilling and upskilling talent. Computers have always been good at keeping data and crunching through it faster than the human brain. Automation of low-risk repetitive tasks can enable humans to focus on parts of their roles that add more value. Robotic Process Automation (RPA), BPMS, and Low Code tools create the flywheel effect of liberating people from repetitive tasks and less interesting work. And now, AI technologies act analytically based on the inputs they receive, making the need for human 'real intelligence' even more important - skills like communication, emotional intelligence, collaboration, empathy, ethics, etc. And as AI makes more complex decisions, humans must be able to ask questions with more cognitive skills.

Platforms and Ecosystem

With the evolution of technology and webs of interlinked value chains, the world is moving toward a 'Platform Economy.' Earlier products and/or services were created and sold by a producer or re-seller to a consumer or business customer. Now people expose a piece of the value chain and get consumers to use that. They become part of the platform and this grows into an ecosystem. Boundaries start disappearing, making it easier for two user groups to generate network value for each other, resulting in mutual benefits that drive the demand-side economies of scale. Platforms provide and monetize the network that connects producers and their ecosystem partners with consumers and business customers. The platform facilitates transactions between participants, and the participants create value via the network effect. The more parties in the ecosystem, the more value consumers can derive from the platform - both as a participant and as an owner.

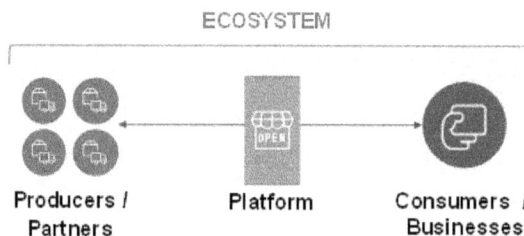

ECOSYSTEM

Producers /   Platform   Consumers /
Partners   Businesses

An ecosystem is the network of such players who work together to define, build, and execute market-creating consumer solutions. An ecosystem is defined by the depth and breadth of potential collaboration among a set of players, and each can deliver a piece of the consumer solution or contribute a necessary capability.

Companies then engage in different revenue models depending on the value proposition they bring to the ecosystem, such as:

- **ADVERTISING** - Offer access to users to advertisers. E.g., Google
- **SUBSCRIPTION** - Pay a fixed amount per month to access the service. E.g., Netflix
- **TRANSACTIONS** - Pay a share or fixed amount per transaction. E.g., Paypal
- **PAY-AS-YOU-GO** - Pay for what you use. E.g., Microsoft Azure
- **FREEMIUM** - Offer a free version with limited features with options for a paid version with more features. E.g., Zoom, Dropbox

The five main guiding principles for companies to play in this ecosystem are:

1. **Be Customer-Led and Data-Driven:** Start with the customer. Use immersive research and combine quantitative and qualitative insight to derive meaningful insights that drive your product design.
2. **Be Value Obsessed:** Focus on identifying and articulating value right from concept through to execution, evolving from value cases.
3. **Co-Create and Collaborate:** The best solutions are co-created with you, your clients, and related stakeholders. It's not

"us versus them" and not first-to-market, but "first-to-scale" that matters in this environment.

4. **Make it Real:** Concepts are brought to life early on through prototyping for constant feedback.

5. **Think Big, Start Small, and then Scale Fast:** Define the vision and the end-state service concept, identify the Minimum Lovable Platform (MLP) for launch, and as the seed germinates, think of scale in areas like talent acquisition, governance, etc.

The HOW - Modern Engineering for Multispeed Agility

Another term we see everywhere is "agile organization." Ever since the Silicon Valley companies glamorized the idea of leanness and agility in a company, IT functions as well as business functions have been trying it out with varying degrees of success. Agile methodology was developed to allow a team to be more responsive to ever-evolving customer requirements while delivering a project. An agile model can allow companies to validate hypotheses and pivot based on customer interactions and timely insights. The initial focus was to build with agility (development) and then move to maintenance with agility (operations), leading to an area called DevOps. Now, agile organizations have learned that even business operations need to be involved in this to enable true agile product management for what the customers want, thereby creating truly lean organizations (BizOps).

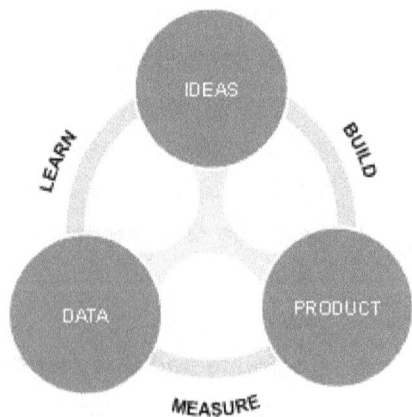

The important takeaway here is that you need to adapt to a multi-speed operating model - the front-end office can be nimble and fast while the back-office operations can still offer stability and do not entail aggressive experimentation. Again, let's use the example of the WeChat super app by Tencent. The front end is trying to be a FinTech provider and there is no boilerplate framework to engage the ever-changing customer tastes. So for a banking function of origination, they can afford to have an architecture that can be torn down quickly if things need to change (trial and error and fail fast). But the backend systems like risk, credit monitoring, and serving functions need robustness and may not need as much change. The typical constraint for a back-office function is capacity, and that can be fulfilled by an appropriate cloud strategy. The middle office is the digital fabric - areas like CRM, ERP, field service, etc. This is called digital decoupling, and a robust API strategy will help companies define this value proposition.

The WHO - Transformation is Still about Culture

The last component of digital transformation lies in the operating fabric of the company. This consists of culture (norms, motivations, behaviors, values, etc.), structures, teams, jobs, roles, and more. Many organizations introducing new digital initiatives or undergoing transformation feel that the *installation* of their new systems, processes, and/or people will mean *adoption* by the organization. They feel that the majority of the work is getting these digitized and digital systems ready. But all too often, even when these initiatives are properly installed, the return expected from the investments does not occur because these changes are not adopted. It is one thing to install a new CRM system for customer intimacy, but totally another to enable the internal and external sales force to adopt and use these systems to offer a view to the customer when that customer touchpoint happens. The human element is key in it on all levels - collaboration, ecosystems, skills, culture, and empowerment.

In the past, business requirements drove technology which then enabled the business to advance with the objective of digitizing processes and making products available through digital channels.

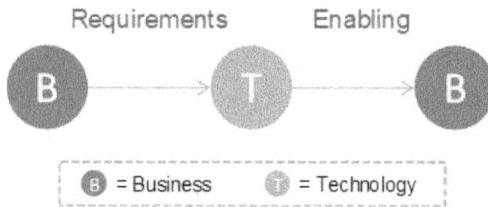

Today, technology creates new opportunities and fundamentally changes businesses and transforms the business and operating models of almost every company in every industry.

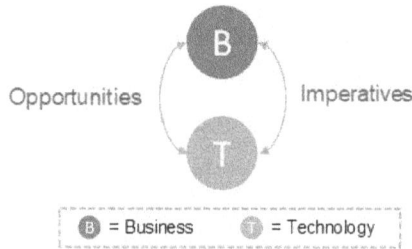

Business Case Aligned to Outcomes

The challenge many companies face is planning a roadmap of investments to ensure that the digital journey enables speed-to-value. Understanding the key value levers needed by the company, aligning those to the corporate strategy, and measuring outcomes to those will enable operational discipline for execution.

Digital transformation initiatives typically belong somewhere on the following value tree:

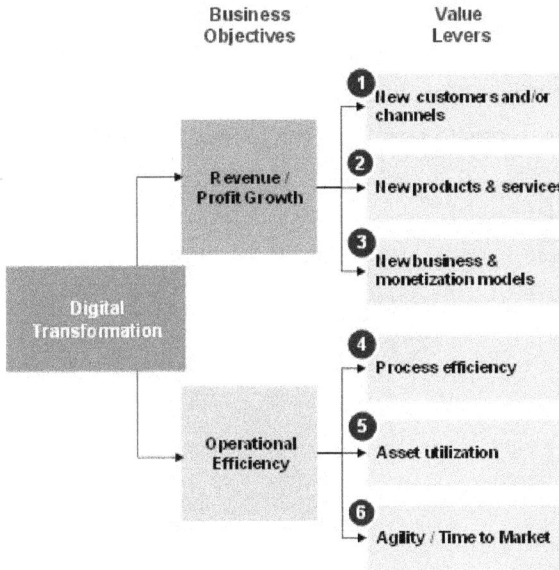

Summary

So, as a recap, the idea of digital transformation is, at its core, all about 'transformation' - both for the customer experience and the employee experience. The current global crisis (due to the pandemic) has mandated a strategic imperative on almost all businesses to accelerate their digital agenda around two dimensions. One is about 'digitizing' the processes, supply chains, and operations to improve the bottom line. This requires more than intelligent automation - these capabilities need to be embedded in the day-to-day work to enable workforce transformation and employee experience (EX). And the other much-talked-about dimension is the focus on customer experience (CX) for revenue growth - the creation of new digital channels and products with due diligence on prioritizing the right S-curve disruptions of existing businesses. This involves incorporating a culture where the voice of the customer is looked at every touchpoint to offer a better experience.

A truly digital business considers both and evaluates existing competitive advantage, industry dynamics, and future trends in consumer tastes to create and scale these new capabilities.

CHAPTER 3

BREAKING THROUGH THE 'GLASS DOOR'

By **BRIAN R. PATRICK**

As a 1970s child growing up in the Bronx, I remember spending my afternoons looking out my 9th-floor living room window at all the people and cars hustling about the Grand Concourse and listening to the cheers from every home game at Yankee Stadium a few blocks away. It was a safe space where I could observe other people without having to interact with them. In 1978, when my dad moved us out to the Long Island suburbs, my shut-in outlook carried on through elementary and middle school. I formed a habit of not raising my hand in class, not participating in group projects, and being the quiet kid picked last for sports teams or forced to watch from the sidelines. My glass window view of the world made me a spectator to everything important, safely separated from those who strived to achieve and sometimes failed. I learned not to ask for help and accept only what came easily or defaulted to me.

Then, there's my race. I have always understood what it means to be black in groups of mostly white people. I never figured out what it means for me to be black by myself. So, I was never fully comfortable in my own skin. I was a shy and quiet child. Once in a while, someone less shy would walk over to me in the playground to say hi and we'd become friends. When I saw someone sitting alone or picked on or hurt, I didn't have the courage to stand up for them, but I would sit next to them. Even if they didn't want to talk or be friends, I'd just stay there so they wouldn't be alone.

As one of the only black students in my high school and growing up in a predominantly white neighborhood, I made friends, but never really felt like I belonged. I continued to feel like some invisible barrier was standing between me and the rest of the world. So, I tried to break through and smash it by doing impressive things that transcended my race. I started earning better grades, made the Honor Roll, won county and state academic competitions in business management, and was written up in the school newsletter for other accomplishments. But all of that didn't change the simple fact that there was a profile for the typical student, the popular guy who was nominated for Prom King or voted 'most likely to succeed,' and I would never fit that profile because I wasn't like most of the group.

I attended Baruch College in the late 1980s, where I spent years cutting class and maxing out credit cards to buy expensive suits and briefcases and eating at restaurants I couldn't afford. I spent all of my money to look like a Wall Street yuppie on the path to success - I even got an unpaid internship with Shearson Lehman Hutton just to look the part of someone who belonged. But this was a fantasy that cost me thousands of dollars and heavy damage to my credit rating when I struggled to pay my bills on time. And none of my college peers made me feel accepted when I couldn't join them for lunch or was in danger of flunking out and needed a friend to talk to. I found myself watching them from afar as I did from my childhood 9th story window. At the time, I didn't have a name for it; now I call this *cohortism*.

I define 'cohortism' or 'cohort mentality' as the phenomenon when a group of people is categorized based on some common-alities— race, gender, income level, education, region, body type, or any other characteristics. Unlike prejudice or bias, the main purpose of cohortism is to provide something to or elicit something from the group for some positive outcome.

Colleges and universities organize students into cohorts based on their year of study. It's the traditional way the faculty determines which courses a student should be required to take first and what minimum cumulative GPA they should maintain based on their experience. Women, People of Color, LGBTQ+: these are cohort names society uses to figure out who we are, where we 'belong,' and what mutual expectations should be set. And all of this calculus happens within seconds, without anyone actually meeting any of us. When you think about it, it is miraculous that any of us succeed in life with so many figures of authority judging us by our cohort type. A pre-set of presumptions which default to an approval or rejection within sec-onds of meeting someone. We are all guilty of this at some point.

It took me years to let go of my feelings of rejection - I was for-tunate to meet new people who are true friends and accept me for who I am. When I rejected cohortism as the road to acceptance, I realized something life-changing: I saw my inner value as a human being because of my diversity, not in spite of it. I stopped trying to meet society's standards. I became my own standard. This led me to go back to school, earn my associate's degree on the Dean's List, get accepted as a transfer student at Columbia University, and earn my Bachelor of Arts in Nonfiction Writing while in my mid-forties. I did this at night while working in a demanding IT career and bootstrap-ping funds to launch my company, GREENLIGHT, Inc.

I have no delusions about myself or why I am writing this - I'm a black man from Generation X who spent my career growing and evolving as part of the African-American business community and now that my generation is turning 50, I want my story to be heard by the Baby Boomers who came before me and the Millennials who will take over after me. I experienced hardship as a person of color striving to be taken seriously and advance in Big Tech. But from the job rejections as well as on-the-job criticisms, I was inspired and compelled to transform every lesson I learned into a continuous improvement system for startups.

I implemented an early version of this system - now called SmartStart™ - to help a former employer attract a $1.2 billion acquisition by Microsoft in 2008. Over the next several years, I evolved this system into the CRUCIBLE Training Scenario platform, which enables innovative and diverse startups to assess, improve, and simulate their management capabilities through wargame-style role play. Early adopters include low-cost college carpooling services like Wheeli.us that reduces our carbon footprint, and mobile communications solutions like Project OWL, which provides first responders in Puerto Rico with life-saving logistical support.

The cohort mentality, however, is still a barrier blocking progress for many of us, especially women and people of color. The barrier is so transparent that we don't notice it until we smack into it. So, we have to be aware of its presence, gauge its thickness, and - like a home contractor - break the glass at its weakest point. If you're female or a person of color striving for a leadership role, you already know about the 'glass ceiling' and how senior management at most companies is still white-male-dominated. So, it makes sense that increasing numbers of aspiring women and minorities have broken away from

Corporate America to start their own companies. But these founders face this cohort mentality as a 'glass door' blocking them from getting the investment funding they need. According to a Deloitte survey of 200+ firms, fewer than 6% of VC investment partners are African American or Latino. Women make up 45% of the VC workforce, but only 14% are investment partner-level. As a group, women and people of color only get about 10% of all venture capital deals.

For years, I have mentored racially diverse cohorts of startup founders to obtain funding. The glass door I refer to is the bias that results in only 10% of all venture funding going to women and entrepreneurs of color. As a group, we are disproportionately being left out of creating new jobs, industry innovations, and billions of dollars of economic growth for underserved communities. For any startup founder who may be facing racial or gender bias in finding investors, here are five techniques to break through that glass door.

Technique #1: Expose investor bias as a blind spot in your pitches.

Richard Kerby, an African American investment partner with Equal Ventures, studied ~1,500 other VC investors and found that 40% are alumni from either Harvard or Stanford and 58% of them are white men. If you want to disrupt this reality, then don't be afraid to acknowledge this in your investor pitches. Tell them that entrepreneurs of color like you don't find many investment firms with diverse or inclusive workplaces and that you believe they are different.

Put them on the spot to be a better version of themselves - you don't really have much to lose since the odds are stacked against you. Do the research and reference other successful founders with your background who beat the odds because investors gave them a chance. Show them the opportunity cost of not investing in your firm based on correlative data between racial or gender homogeneity and disproportionate investments for female and racially diverse startups. Display a chart of estimated annual returns they didn't receive because they have a blind spot to firms like yours.

By bringing this to their attention in your pitch, you'll force the potential investors to examine their own biases and they are more likely to give you a chance.

Technique #2: Nurture your credit profiles and seek alternate funding sources.

Sometimes you can't get an angel investor at the beginning and you have to bootstrap your startup - I experienced that challenge myself. Like many small businesses, I had to apply for business credit cards, and I would never have qualified if I had not worked so hard to improve my FICO scores with timely payments over the years. This is even more critical for female entrepreneurs. A 2018 report from Biz2Credit determined the average FICO score of female entrepreneurs was 588 compared to 613 of male founders. The report went further by stating female entrepreneurs are 5% less likely to obtain business loans than men. Female founders receive 1.3% of their financing from venture capital and typically give up more equity stake and management control during negotiations for private funding than their male counterparts.

Technique #3: Stop sabotaging your own pitch.

Investors may be picking up signals of uncertainty or doubt during pitches with female founders and overall, women receive about 5% less funding than men. HSBC's Global Private Bank commissioned a report titled "She's The Business" to explore the investment challenges faced by over 1,200 female entrepreneurs. 54% of female entrepreneurs in the United Kingdom and 46% in the United States reported potentially gender-biased questions concerning their personal and family circumstances, their self-perception of their leadership ability, and their credibility. 68% of female entrepreneurs surveyed felt confident during the pitch process, but later, ranked confidence as the top area they want to improve.

Most of the female responses in this research were more introspective, self-critical, and less optimistic regarding their investment pitch. Now I'm not saying that women should pretend to be aloof and feign total confidence to get funding, but there's nothing wrong with suspending self-criticism before and during a pitch. I created a training platform for startup founders called the CRUCIBLE Training Scenario to assess management competency with our SmartStart™ scoring, improve capability with a continuous improvement plan, and simulate success using boot camp-style scenarios.

Technique #4: Reference successful entrepreneurs from your demographic who they overlooked.

Based on the correlation between racial and gender homogeneity of managing partners at venture capital funds and the lower number of women and minorities receiving funding from these institutions, we can infer that there is a bias loop where young white males continue to get more money because they are the vast majority of success stories. This self-fulfilling prophecy marginalizes female and minority prospects, amplifying their risk profile in the minds of venture capital investors.

But a deeper treatment of this issue leads to a need to reevaluate the definition of 'success' in various types of businesses. A key metric for a tech startup may not be comparable with that for a yoga practice; it's like apples to oranges. Another disadvantage is company size. Women tend to start more sole proprietorships with fewer employees, which skews the numbers. According to the Association of Women's Business Centers, almost 90% of female-owned businesses have only one employee (the founder).

In order to combat this bias, it is important to show the potential investors examples of successful entrepreneurs and companies led by people with your background and from your demographic. This helps the investors see your potential and not just compare you to the white male entrepreneurs they may have invested in previously. It also adds social proof to your business idea.

Technique #5: Pursue 'impact investors' who embrace your diversity.

In short, 'impact investing' is a trend toward identifying and rewarding businesses which provide the maximum benefit to underserved communities, enabling a stronger ecosystem and enhanced sustainability. This approach is not widely accepted yet, but McKinsey forecasts impact investing will increase to $300 billion by 2020. Furthermore, there are some investors of color who are hitting against and breaking through the glass door to funding.

When Arlan Hamilton, Founder and Managing Partner of Backstage Capital, spoke at a 2019 Columbia Organization of Rising Entrepreneurs (CORE) event to a packed audience, she explained how she began cracking the glass door by creating her own VC fund dedicated to impact funding. When she mentioned her upcoming book, *It's About Damn Time*, she added, "We invest in the very best founders who identify as women, people of color, or LGBTQ. I personally identify as all three."

Four other venture capitalists of color - Brandon Bryant, Jarrid Tingle, Henri Pierre-Jacques, and John Henry - have partnered up to create Harlem Capital, with the goal of funding up to 1,000 female and minority founders by 2040. They compiled a database of 200 racially diverse investors for founders to network with for funding deals they may not receive from predominantly white male firms. Impact investors will help female and minority founders to obtain VC funding by assessing and improving their capabilities with targeted coaching and simulated role-play. They combat the funding gap by matching diverse entrepreneurs with fellow investors dedicated to supporting underserved communities.

But there is still much work to be done. When I consulted with Jean-Pierre Adechi, the Haitian-American CEO and Founder of Wheeli.us - a college ridesharing service - his firm raised a total of $100K in funding over two rounds; their latest funding was raised on October 26, 2018, from a seed round. In contrast, Uber has raised a total of $24.7B in funding over 23 rounds and Lyft has raised a total of $4.9B in funding over 20 rounds. If you compare all three of their business models, Wheeli.us is just as viable with much lower overhead, faster scalability, and a more compelling message on reducing our carbon footprint by carpooling and making new college friends along the way. The investment community still views Uber and Lyft as the standard-bearer for their industry and their co-founders fit the cohort mentality for success. While Uber and Lyft have already had IPOs, Jean-Pierre's founders get overlooked for follow-on funding.

To move forward, all our perceptions and perspectives must undergo a change. My own did years ago. The glass door to women and minority entrepreneurs is still there and it's just like my old 9th story window when I was a child. But this time, I'm on the outside looking in.

References:

As Revenue of Women-Owned Businesses Rose, Credit Scores Dropped in 2018. https://www.biz2credit.com/research-reports/as-revenue-of-women-owner-businesses-rose-credit-scores-dropped-in-2018. Accessed 19 Feb. 2020.

Association of Women's Business Centers. https://irp-cdn.multiscreensite.com/fb72abcb/files/uploaded/ccfwib.pdf. Accessed 19 Feb. 2020.

Diversity in Venture Capital - NVCA-Deloitte Human Capital Survey Dashboard | Deloitte US. https://www2.deloitte.com/content/campaigns/us/audit/survey/diversity-venture-capital-human-capital-survey-dashboard.html. Accessed 19 Feb. 2020.

Gowthaman, Nirandhi. "She's the Business - HSBC Study Reveals Women Entrepreneurs Face Gender Bias When Seeking Funding." YourStory.Com, 11 Oct. 2019, https://yourstory.com/herstory/2019/10/hsbc-study-women-entrepreneurs-gender-bias-less-funding.

Understanding Impact Investing | McKinsey. https://www.mckinsey.com/industries/private-equity-and-principal-investors/our-insights/a-closer-look-at-impact-investing. Accessed 19 Feb. 2020.

"Venture Capital's Diversity Disaster." TechCrunch, http://social.techcrunch.com/2018/07/30/venture-capitals-diversity-disaster/. Accessed 19 Feb. 2020.

CHAPTER 4

CREATING YOUR DREAM RETIREMENT

By **BRUCE ELFENBEIN**

I have a proposition for you. We become partners. *You* put up all of the money. *You* run the business on a day-to-day basis, deal with vendors, human resources, receivables, health insurance, and everything else involved in running the business. Then one day, I'll show up and tell you how much you owe me. Can I get a show of hands for how many people want to get into business with me?

Most of you already have a partner just like that. His name is Uncle Sam. If you have a 401(k) or an IRA, then that above scenario describes your business relationship. That is why it's important to apply advanced tax strategies to the money you've worked so hard for. It's not just what you make, it's what you get to keep.

My feelings about qualified retirement plans are mixed. These plans were created for the companies that run the plans to make money. You? Not so much. Don't get me wrong, they don't mind if you make money, too. Honestly, they prefer it since it keeps your contributions flowing. However, limited choices and fees, both those they are legally required to disclose and hidden fees, often total between 5% to 6% annually. If the stock market averages an 8% return, you are lucky to get a 2% or 3% return after fees are deducted. Beating those costs are an uphill battle, even with an employer's matching contributions.

Yet, the vast majority of those who seek my advice on retirement or advanced tax planning bring that as either their sole or largest retirement asset. Hence, my mixed feelings. If it wasn't for their 401(k) or IRA, they would have almost nothing saved.

So, let's talk about retirement planning. Most people only focus on saving and accumulation. That's okay during your working years, but your broker may not have the expertise required for the next phase: distribution.

While you never stop your accumulation, you need to factor in a number of different variables here: taxes, inflation, market risk, sequence of returns risk, chronic illness risk, healthcare costs, and longevity. Quite the laundry list of needs, right?

Overwhelming. Confusing. Can I get a root canal instead? I would prefer to plan my own funeral rather than plan my retirement. These are common sentiments I encounter when putting together a working plan for one's retirement. I've heard the cliché that we spend more time planning for a vacation than we do planning our retirement. They are not that dissimilar, except that one lasts the rest of your life.

I get it. We not only have to figure out how to make our savings and investments last a lifetime, but we also have to plan for the obstacles and risks along the way, such as creating a guaranteed income stream. If you make a mistake along the way, it could be devastating.

While it can be easier (and recommended) to hire a trusted professional, such as a Certified Financial Fiduciary® (you can find one at www.nationalcffassociation.org), there are always a number of do-it-yourselfers who want to tackle it alone. Besides, even with professional assistance, I believe it is important to understand the process and the components involved.

The Basics of Retirement Planning

We'll start with the basics and adjust our plan from there. You must understand that, by nature, your plan must be flexible and able to adjust according to changes in your situation. That's the hallmark of a good plan.

Your first step is to establish how much you spend every month. Be honest with yourself and be as accurate as possible. If you need a little help with this, there are a number of monthly budget worksheets online, or you can use the one at the end of this chapter. It comes from The American Financial Education Alliance (an excellent non-profit organization) and I find it to be a very good template. Once you have that number, you're on your way. Now we know how much we need.

The next step is to add up all of your sources of **GUARANTEED INCOME.** Guaranteed income. Those are the two magic words that determine the quality of your life in retirement. Everything, and I mean everything, is based on your guaranteed income. Guaranteed income can include your Social Security benefits, any pension payments, annuity payments, interest payments, rental property pay-ments, income from bonds, CD's, etc. You may notice an exclusion here, and that is income from your portfolio. Why is that not included? Simple. It's not guaranteed. We'll get into that a little later.

So, now we need to do a little math here. Get a calculator if you must. Subtract your average monthly expenses from your monthly **guaranteed income.** If you have a positive number, then congratulations. You are on your way to a great retirement. If your number is negative, then we need to make up that gap. This is going to be our baseline or starting point.

Let's look at a couple of examples:

Ralph and Alice live a reasonable lifestyle, with expenses totaling about $4000.00 per month. Ralph is a retired bus driver and receives a pension from the city of $2500.00 per month and has a Social Security benefit of $1800.00 per month. Alice, a retired legal secretary, doesn't have a pension but does have a healthy 401k balance of $350,000.00 and a Social Security benefit of $1200.00 per month. Their combined **guaranteed income** is $5500.00 per month. That leaves them an excess of $1500.00 per month, which can be used to improve their lifestyle, invest, or go into savings. Ralph and Alice are looking pretty good at this point. They can even afford that dream cruise sponsored by the International Order of Loyal Raccoons.

Ralph's best friend and neighbor, Ed, and his wife Trixie are a different story. Ed was a Public Works employee until he got injured and was placed on disability. That reduced income for Ed and Trixie put them in the hole, as it was not quite enough to cover their monthly expenses of $4000.00 per month. This required them to dip into their savings every month. Trixie just retired from her job working at a dry cleaner, earning about $1500.00 per month. Ed's disability of $2000.00 per month and Trixie's salary gave them a combined income of only $3500.00 per month, leaving them short by $500.00 per month, which was quickly eroding their nest egg.

Since Ed just turned 66, he received some not-so-great news. His disability was ending, and his Social Security benefit was kicking in automatically, which was going to remain at $2000.00 per month. This issue was compounded by Trixie's Social Security benefit of only $800.00 per month, which gave them a combined guaranteed income of only $2800.00 per month, leaving them a shortfall or gap of $1200.00 per month.

What are their choices? Keep working or cut expenses by down-sizing their home. (There's always lottery scratch off tickets. But I guess if that really worked, more people would be doing that, so......no) Or Ed and Trixie needed to find a way to leverage whatever assets they have in order to close the gap.

Ed was not what you would call a sophisticated investor. He once invested in Herkamore technology. However, about 15 years ago, Ed purchased a fixed indexed annuity, a guaranteed retirement income product, and contributed to that every paycheck. It had grown to over $400,000.00. Today, he could turn on income like turning on a faucet and receive a guaranteed income of over $20,000.00 a year, for the rest of his life…while his money continued to grow. Now that's what I call leverage!

So, because Ed made a wise choice, they will be alright. In fact, they'll be able to join Ralph and Alice on that dream cruise sponsored by the International Order of Loyal Raccoons.

Does that mean an annuity is the right product for your situation? Maybe. This is not a "pitch" to sell you an annuity. But there are a lot of great financial instruments out there (and some not so great). It's just finding the right ones for your specific situation.

"Sometimes I feel that designing the perfect retirement plan is like putting together a 5000-piece puzzle, where all of the pieces are white…on both sides."
–ANONYMOUS

Stock Market Investments are Not Guaranteed

Let's talk about the stock market. Why don't I include it with guaranteed income? First, it's not guaranteed. Your account goes up and down. What if you need the money when it's down? The percentage of drawdown (with a 94% certainty) that you can safely take without fear of running out of money is only 3%. Think about that for a moment.

Suppose you have an account with one million dollars in it. That means, in retirement, to ensure that you will not run out of money, you can only withdraw $30,000.00 annually. I work with millionaires on a daily basis. To think that they have achieved that goal usually means that they have a standard of living that will not be totally supported by that amount.

One of the reasons for this is what we call the "Sequence of Returns" risk. Take a look at the below chart. On the left, we start with the same amount but have simply reversed the sequence of returns. As you can see, with no withdrawals, the sequence of returns has no bearing on our final account value. However, on the right, we are withdrawing 5% per year for living expenses. Here, the sequence of returns really matters, and it makes a huge difference, where in one instance, those withdrawals mean we run out of money in a few years.

| | Annual Income = None | | | | | Annual Income = 5% of first-year value adjusted for inflation | | | |
| | Starting Value for Portfolio A and Portfolio B = $100,000 | | | | | Starting Value for Portfolio A and Portfolio B = $684,848 | | | |
Age	Annual Return	Portfolio A Year-End Value	Annual Return	Portfolio B Year-End Value	Age	Annual Return	Portfolio A Year-End Value	Annual Return	Portfolio B Year-End Value
41	-12%	$87,695	29%	$129,491	66	-12%	$566,337	29%	$852,571
42	-21%	$69,426	18%	$152,281	67	-21%	$413,086	18%	$967,355
43	-14%	$59,707	25%	$189,590	68	-14%	$318,927	25%	$1,168,029
44	22%	$72,984	-6%	$178,404	69	22%	$352,432	-6%	$1,061,698
45	10%	$80,136	15%	$204,272	70	10%	$348,431	15%	$1,177,105
46	4%	$83,595	8%	$221,183	71	4%	$323,772	8%	$1,234,855
47	11%	$92,707	27%	$281,124	72	11%	$318,176	27%	$1,525,614
48	3%	$95,210	-2%	$274,939	73	3%	$284,653	-2%	$1,452,871
49	-3%	$92,155	15%	$315,355	74	-3%	$232,143	15%	$1,623,066
50	21%	$111,507	19%	$375,272	75	21%	$236,215	19%	$1,886,771
51	17%	$130,129	33%	$498,737	76	17%	$229,644	33%	$2,461,500
52	5%	$137,026	11%	$554,097	77	5%	$194,417	11%	$2,687,327
53	-10%	$123,597	-10%	$499,795	78	-10%	$126,543	-10%	$2,375,148
54	11%	$137,316	5%	$526,284	79	11%	$90,304	5%	$2,450,746
55	33%	$182,493	17%	$614,174	80	33%	$68,219	17%	$2,808,226
56	19%	$217,167	21%	$743,150	81	19%	$27,833	21%	$3,344,606
57	15%	$249,091	-3%	$719,305	82	15%	$0	-3%	$3,182,338
58	-2%	$243,611	3%	$738,726	83	-2%	$0	3%	$3,211,664
59	27%	$309,629	11%	$819,247	84	27%	$0	11%	$3,503,440
60	8%	$335,262	4%	$854,602	85	8%	$0	4%	$3,594,592
61	15%	$383,875	10%	$938,354	86	15%	$0	10%	$3,885,017
62	-6%	$361,226	22%	$1,147,022	87	-6%	$0	22%	$4,685,527
63	25%	$449,727	-14%	$986,439	88	25%	$0	-14%	$3,963,710
64	18%	$528,878	-21%	$780,941	89	18%	$0	-21%	$3,070,398
65	29%	$684,848	-12%	$684,848	90	29%	$0	-12%	$2,622,984
	8%	$684,848	8%	$684,848		8%	$0	8%	$2,622,984

— No Difference —   — Big Difference —

Sequence of returns risk is different from market risk itself. We invest in the market to make money, right? But we're big boys and girls. We always know that the market goes two ways, up and down. The problem is we don't know when.

Don't get me wrong. I'm not "down" on the market. I have money in the stock market. But in retirement, I use it properly. What do I mean by that? When people ask me what I think the market is going to do tomorrow, I always reply truthfully: "I don't know." "How about next week?" The same answer. "Next year?" Ditto. But how about ten years from now? Yes, the market will be higher than today. How about twenty years from now? Yes, it will be higher then, too.

So, if we know this, then why don't we use the market properly? That is, why not keep a percentage of our assets invested in the market for the future, to help counter the effects of inflation and increased taxes? It works for me and maybe it will work for you as well.

I usually use a basic model when balancing my assets. Most of my assets, approximately 65 to 70%, are in guaranteed income products because we are earning guaranteed rates between 4% and 8% and that's how much I need to invest in order to maintain our standard of living in retirement at those returns.

We keep about 10% liquid in our emergency fund to pay bills and have a ready source of cash in case we need to replace the hot water heater or fix the roof. Here, it is about liquidity, not return, so we are generally earning less than 1%.

Finally, we keep about 20% to 25% invested in the market to account for future inflation and taxes. Even though we like to keep a portion in the market for future growth, we have observed that we have actually gotten a better return on our guaranteed portion, since they never have any losses to recover from or make up for, giving us an additional opportunity cost.

Illness & Injury

Of all of the risks to your retirement funds, I have never witnessed anything more devastating to your assets than a chronic illness. It can turn your nest egg into a scrambled mess quicker than you can imagine. There is greater than a 50% possibility that one member of a couple will require treatment for a chronic illness. Injury is the most common cause.

The time this concern usually pops up is when people have witnessed the effect it has on a friend or a relative and they decide that they do not want that to happen to them. Unfortunately, they often come to that decision too late.

There are a number of different products to address this issue, such as long-term care insurance. Many of my clients have it. No one is unhappy about it, either. It has saved the financial lives of many families. Yet a late realization is not good. By then, most people no longer qualify for it medically or the premiums are so high that they can no longer afford it.

Again, this is not a "pitch" to purchase Long-Term Care insurance. The most important takeaway here is that you need a plan for long-term care if your retirement funds are depleted due to illness or injury. If need be, can you move in with relatives or friends? Do you qualify for any additional government benefits, such as the Veteran's Aid and Attendance benefit or Medicaid?

In some instances, we can go to a fairly recent product innovation known as a "hybrid product," which combines several products into one, such as life insurance and long-term care insurance. Hybrid products have easier underwriting and lower premiums. If you have an injury or illness that requires a stay in a nursing home or in-home care, this will cover you. If not, you leave a hunk of tax-free money behind for your beneficiaries.

Yes, planning for your retirement can be daunting. That is why I always recommend using someone who has expertise in that arena. If you want to do it yourself, then go ahead. There is no shortage of information out there to help you on the way. I hope that this has proved to be of value to you to that end. Good luck and have a beautiful retirement!

Budget Worksheet

Income:	Monthly Amt:
Wages, Salaries & Tips	
Commission	
Bonuses	
Interest Income (Sav, CD, Bonds, etc.)	
Dividends (Stock, MF's, ETF's, etc)	
Gifts (Inheritance, Trust Fund, etc)	
Alimony &/or Child Support	
Penison(s) & Life Annuities	

Income:	Monthly Amt:
Social Security (Spouse 1)	
Social Security (Spouse 2)	
IRA Distributions (Spouse 1)	
IRA Distributions (Spouse 2)	
Rental Property	
Privately Funded Loans	
Other	
Other	

Total Monthly Income	

Expenses: Household	Monthly Amt:
Mortgage Principal & Interest	
Real Estate Taxes	
Rent	
Insurance - Home/Rental	
Maintenance - Supplies	
Utilities - Gas/Electric	
Water - Sewer	
Cable - Phone - Internet	
House Cleaning	
Cell Phones	
Other	
Other	
Total	

Daily Living	Monthly Amt:
Groceries	
Dining - Eating Out	
Clothing - Dry Cleaning - Laundry	
Salon - Massage - Manicure	
Other	
Other	
Total	

Entertainment	Monthly Amt:
Home - Shows - Events	
Sports - Hobbies - Lessons	
Dues - Memberships	
Vacation - Travel	
Other	
Other	
Total	

Total Monthly Expenses	

Total Discretionary Income	

Expenses: Transportation	Monthly Amt:
Auto Loan 1	
Auto Loan 2	
Auto Insurance	
Fuel	
Repairs	
Other	
Other	
Total	

Health	
Health Insurance	
Life Insurance	
LTC Insurance	
Disability Insurance	
Medicine - Drugs	
Veterinarian - Pet Care	
Other	
Other	
Total	

Debts, Loans	
Credit Cards	
Student Loans	
Alimony - Child Support	
Other	
Other	
Total	

Charity, Gifts	
Charitable Donations	
Gifts - Birthday - Christmas	
Other	
Other	
Total	

Please explain any unexpected changes in your income and expenses over the next 20 years:

Income Changes (pensions, expected inheritances, gauranteed income annuities, RMD's – if known, etc.)

_____

_____

_____

_____

_____

_____

_____

_____

_____

_____

Expense Changes (House paid off, other debt paid off, large gists to children, college funding etc.)

_____

_____

_____

_____

_____

_____

_____

_____

_____

_____

CHAPTER 5

COMING SOON TO A CORPORATION NEAR YOU

By **CHRIS REAVIS**

When is the last time a large tech project went incredibly well for you? Was it delivered early, under budget, and with additional features?

For most of us, the answer is "I can't remember" and laughter.

Most of us have come to accept that technical projects deliver late, over budget, and with less functionality than we wanted. This problem is more significant - and more ignored - than you may realize. It's certainly not due to a lack of resources.

According to Gartner, four trillion dollars were spent in 2019 on tech projects. For comparison, this is larger than the total output (GDP) for the United Kingdom's 66 million occupants.

What happens with this massive spend? According to PriceWaterhouseCoopers, only 2.5% of those projects make it to completion.

Imagine, for a moment, how this would compare to everyday things in your life. Using the same percentage, this would mean you would have about nine days each year that you had power, transportation, and water. If this was the case, you would be (rightly) outraged. So, why aren't we outraged at this massive inefficiency with IT projects?

Let's dive in a bit more and talk about cost overruns. According to a study at Harvard, one in six tech projects has cost overruns of 200%. For the rest of them, the average overrun was 27%.

Being that we have put up for this for some time, you may not be shocked. Again though, let's compare this to something real and more practical. What if your grocery bill was suddenly twice as much for the same groceries? Oh, you want to shop somewhere else? You can't. Many IT organizations say you can only get technology services through them.

What are companies doing about this? Are they changing their approaches to improve? Sadly, no. They are spending even more on the same technology, consulting, and project management - even though this continued approach shows a high failure rate.

Clearly, a dangerous belief has permeated most large companies. That belief is that tech efforts are "hard" and problems around tech projects are expensive, unreliable, and late.

The good news for all of us is that this can be successfully detangled. There is a proven, repeatable way to enjoy technical project success. It doesn't require a new technology vendor, consulting firm, reorganization, executive change, architect, project management team, cloud, or tech team. In fact, most companies already have the ingredients they need to make this change successfully.

What We Found

Most leaders are frustrated with the pace of their organizations. They're exhausted by tech projects with bloated costs and budget overruns - and not moving the dial fast enough for their customers.

These leaders are concerned that their organization celebrates mediocrity over innovation, and their organization's fear of change paralyzes them from taking positive action. With COVID-19, they are charged to do even more with less, having to create change in a culture that violently opposes it.

Their organization is often locked in "problem admiration" - dozens of meetings talking about the same issues (again and again) but failing to truly solve them. These meetings often recur around major issues, with a multi-million dollar "solution," a new architecture, and new vendors. When it isn't funded, the teams throw their hands up as if there's very little they can do. Or sometimes worse, it is funded and has the issues we have discussed.

Leaders tell me that their organization often believes they don't have enough. The belief is that if they somehow had more, it would solve the problem. They say they need more tech, specialized staff, better project management, cloud investments, or technical architects.

However, more just never seems to solve the issues. Most leaders I talk with know the real problem is something else - they just aren't sure how to easily define this beast.

The Real Problem

The real problem is the lack of a "results culture." The organization needs to decide that it is easy, detangle the made-up complexities, and find ways to immediately prototype.

Sure, that's easy to say - but does it really work? Will it really work in environments that are hundreds of years old with regulatory issues and all sorts of other considerations?

In a word, yes. Here's one example.

Regulated Energy Company

A large, regulated energy company was spinning off a deregulated portion of the company. They spent over a year planning the technical parts of this with dozens of staff. There were lots of meetings, but not much action. At the time, they were also charging the deregulated company $110k per employee for "fully loaded" technology costs. Some of those charges included forcing them to use technology they despised (SAP, Mainframe, etc.).

Clearly, this situation wasn't acceptable to the new company, and they needed a new approach.

Using our methodology, this spin-off was able to migrate SAP and stand up a new ERP in 90 days. They ran what quickly became a $4B business with just 22 IT employees. This included complex energy trading software, dozens of physical sites, and 500 employees. The new company ended up heavily regulated as well, being in the energy delivery space, and still kept up their efficiencies. And yes, the cost per employee for tech dropped ten-fold.

They made use of a few things that we'll talk about in a moment - including future state focus, assume results, make it easy, brain science, and immediate prototypes. This organization has continued to scale well and was later purchased by a massive international giant.

While this story may seem the exception, these problems are common with all large enterprises today.

What is the Magic Pixie Dust?

IBM used to have TV ads joking about using "magic pixie dust" to solve IT problems. While funny, it seems as if current enterprises are hoping something magical comes along and makes all their pain go away.

While I'm not aware of any such magic dust, my company has created a proven, repeatable, ten-step process that can get organizations back on track quickly.

Let's go through one of our ten approaches briefly here. I'll explain how using a proven brain science approach can immediately unlock your organization's potential.

Brain Science

The technology here is what we call "wetware" - your nervous system.

Remember, your wetware's job is to replay the past and keep you safe. It is concerned about survival. New patterns are a risk and not in the best interest of your survival. Also, your fight/flight/freeze responses are still active. Even though we don't have bears and tigers in our daily lives, our brain still treats everyday stressors this way. That has a massive impact on our lives and choices.

When we are in that stressed state, our brain goes into the fight/flight/freeze response automatically. In that state, other parts of our brain are literally turned off. Think of turning off the electric breaker box in your house. Lights don't turn on because there's no current going there. In fight/flight/freeze, your primitive brain is the breaker box, and your reasoning, logic, and problem-solving are turned off. They aren't available.

Okay, what does this have to do with tech projects? More than you think.

We'll get into a specific methodology here in a moment, but first some science. Over 50 years of brain science at Harvard have found that you can help people come out of fight/flight/freeze with empathy. Yes, this has been scientifically proven and is evidence-based. Small, consistent doses of empathy get people out of fight/flight/freeze - and even better, get people into being able to use problem-solving skills in their cortex.

Try this experiment for a week: Ask major stakeholders and those directly involved about a technical problem at your company. Do this one-on-one and live (call, in person, or video conference).

It's very important to do this in a specific way and order for the best results.

Here are eight proven steps:

1. Ask to meet in a neutral place - coffee, lunch, or similar. Don't do this in an office or cubicle, and ideally not in a conference room. Obviously, during COVID-19, this is an online meeting or call.

2. Start the conversation with something like, "Hey, listen you aren't in trouble here - it seems like project XYZ has some issues, what's going on?"

3. Now your job is to **listen**. Let's be clear: this doesn't mean planning your next statement or argument. It means listening. Take notes. Listening also means confirming what they are saying, such as "Okay, so the spec was way off? That makes sense, it was frustrating..." It's your job to validate what they say - even if you don't agree with it - so they feel heard.

4. After a while, ask something like, "I get where you are coming from. Do you feel heard?" If they say, yes, you continue, if not, then you keep listening. **Pro tip:** *You may be listening for a few sessions before you move forward. That's okay.*

5. Once you get the go-ahead that they feel heard, your next step is to ask to share your concerns. "I totally understand your perspective. I'd like to share my concern, is that okay? (yes) My concern is meeting our timeline/budget/scope."

6. You then ask if your concern makes sense to them. Yes, your concern has to be simplified and stated in a word or two. You may not receive massive empathy back - keep going.

7. Here's where more magic happens. Ask the person for their ideas to resolve the situation. You will hear a lot of things - just listen again and say something like, "That's an idea to consider." Take notes. You are listening again and not judging the ideas.

8. If there's one or two ideas that also work for you, ask at the end if you can work with them on this together, and check in on it again next week.

What Just Happened?

You just led someone who was locked into a corporate fight/flight/freeze response into being able to problem-solve. This process actually lights up different neural pathways, so this person won't get stuck. You've also strengthened the relationship and continued to build trust with them.

Yes, it can feel a little strange at first, that's for sure, and maybe you think this is too simple to work. However, this proven method will unlock the potential of those you work with like nothing I've ever seen. My challenge to you is to try it for a week or two and see what happens to your deliverables, budget, and timeline. In every client we have ever worked with, they have had phenomenal results, even though it felt weird at first.

But Wait, I Want More

If you are ready to take your career and organization to the next level, we have a proven approach to get you there.

This approach includes a creative intake method, sharing our proven methodology, practical online classes, one-on-one coaching, and an executive presentation. We cover technical and non-technical skills to make sure your tech projects hit their scope, timeline, and budget goals - every time.

Our classes and coaching topics include how to use a future state focus, use what you already have, assuming results, prototype rapidly, play by the rules and still be a maverick, detangle and make it easy, targeted collaboration, applied empathy, and more.

We take you through this step-by-step, so you can enjoy practical results. In a few months, you'll shape your tech projects from medi-ocre to stellar. You'll be able to help your company better serve its customers, and be known for getting things done. This is a recipe for company success and your career growth.

If you are ready to take this to the next level, reach out now on the web or drop me an email (avidintent.com or chris@avidintent.com). We'll get on the phone together and get you set up for success.

We are looking forward to working with change agents like you and celebrating your triumphs!

CHAPTER 6

HOW MOONSHOTS CREATE
NEW MARKETS

By **ERIC AGUILAR**

When I was fresh out of Cal Poly with a degree in Electrical and Electronics Engineering in my hands, I had no idea what I wanted to pursue. Like many recent college graduates, I had a lot of ideas but no specific direction yet.

I ended up getting a Systems Engineer position at Raytheon, an international defense contractor. There, I began my career creating and building sensors for drones.

Sensors are fascinating technology because they allow us to observe the world around us. The first sensors I built were radar receivers built from the silicon level. During testing, the sensors were performing extremely well with sensing moving vehicles but we couldn't figure out why they were having trouble recognizing parked and non-moving vehicles.

A mentor of mine told me about a research study showing how our eyes dither to help identify and extract still objects. Dithering is when your eyes vibrate in your eye sockets. In recordings of eyes, you can clearly see constant small vibrations. Taking inspiration from nature, we applied dithering to our radar system to make our sensors vibrate and there was an immediate significant improvement in the image quality of the sensors. It was very exciting.

Since that revelation, I have constantly looked to nature for ways to solve real-world technology issues when developing and integrating sensors, now for autonomous vehicles. After working with drones, I moved into the self-driving car space. Drones and autonomous cars are directly correlated. With drones, you're creating something to fly autonomously and using programming, sensors, algorithms, and new technology to allow the drones to learn and map out an environment. Self-driving cars have the same fundamental needs in a more complex form.

My experience working in sensors and other technology gave me insight into just how much invention and innovation is still needed to bring natural capabilities to robots and self-driving cars.

Since my first job out of college at Raytheon, I have since worked for other innovative tech companies, such as being an Avionics Lead at Google X, a Firmware and Integration Lead at Tesla working on the Model 3, and as the Sensor Lead at Argo AI.

That first experience incorporating a nature-inspired solution to a technological problem motivated and inspired me to find more solutions in nature. In early 2019, I co-founded and am the CEO of Omnitron Sensors, where we enable full autonomy with novel silicon photonics processes for sensors in safety-critical systems. The direct inspiration for starting Omnitron came from an issue with LIDAR sensors in self-driving cars. Every autonomous car has a few of these LIDAR sensors, but they are extremely expensive - up to $100,000 each! And while the cost is exorbitant, the bigger issue is reliability. The six-figure sensors were breaking after only three to six months, needing to be replaced and recalibrated often. This was not sustainable, and every hour fixing, replacing, and recalibrating was lost revenue.

This issue is not found in nature. Our eyes track moving objects and the brain deals with the movement and vibration by compensating for it. We have a sophisticated closed-loop system around the eye to track things and through the inner ear to compensate for vibration and motion, and Omnitron is applying those same natural solutions and principles to the scanner for LIDAR sensors.

My company is one of many to derive from the technology needed to drive forward the self-driving car revolution. The push for just one big idea - an autonomous car - expands the entire industry and a ton of derivative and supporting technology emerges creating whole new industries.

New Demands in Technology Create New Innovations

The demands of autonomous vehicles, the next moonshot, and their needs have created a host of new technologies and innovations in existing technologies, which has led to the creation and acquisition of new tech companies.

Some excellent examples of innovations born from the self-driving car revolution include NVIDIA, which had several thousand engineers working for years to develop the V100 chip. The V100 chip provides the first high-performance graphics processor used in self-driving and was inspired by Elon Musk's need for auto-pilot technology. Since creating the V100 chip, NVIDIA has become a leader in artificial intelligence technology for self-driving cars.

Another example is Mobileye, a technology company for sensor fusion, mapping, and front- and rear-facing camera technology. Mobileye has a sensor and processor combination which offers the most advanced driver-assistance capabilities pushing the envelope in how much a car can truly drive itself. Their innovations caught the attention of Intel, who acquired Mobileye in 2017 for $15.3 billion in the largest-ever acquisition of an Israeli tech company.

There have been a number of acquisitions and developments of LIDAR companies by self-driving car giants, too. LIDAR stands for Light Detection and Ranging and is a remote sensing method that uses light in the form of a pulsed laser to measure variable distances. LIDAR builds a map of the world around the sensor by shooting out millions of light pulses per second and measuring how long it takes for the light to come back. Unlike cameras, LIDAR systems do not rely on ambient light and see with better precision than radar. In May 2017, ABI Research, a technology research firm, released information saying they expect the value of the LIDAR market to get to $13 billion by 2027. This just goes to show the immense value in the derivative technologies coming from the self-driving car market.

General Motors self-driving car startup, Cruise, acquired Strobe LIDAR, a Pasadena-based startup making what could be a key technology to self-driving cars in fleets. Strobe's technology is ideally going to reduce the cost of making the sensors GM needs by up to 99 percent.

Ford is another large car company investing in autonomous vehicle technology. In 2017, Ford subsidiary Argo AI acquired Princeton Lightwave specifically for its LIDAR technology after investing in Velodyne in 2016. Lightwave's sensor is based around a Geiger-mode avalanche photodiode (APD), a component that detects the photons bouncing off objects around the sensor, and is sensitive enough to detect a single photon.

More recently, in May 2019, Aurora, a self-driving car startup founded in 2017 and backed by industry giants Sequoia Capital and Amazon, acquired Blackmore. Blackmore is a LIDAR company based in Bozeman, Montana, and is one of the few companies developing frequency-modulated continuous-wave LIDAR (FMCW). Most of the LIDAR companies now are still developing AM LIDAR sensors to form 3D maps. FMCW uses a low-power continuous wave of light and can measure distance with a higher dynamic range and instant velocity, meaning it can measure the speed of objects.

The Push for Self-Driving Has Created New Industries & Markets

Industries and markets that didn't exist 15 or 30 years ago are now major players pushing the envelope and creating whole new markets.

Some new industries born from this include warehouse robotics and automation, security robotics, and even agricultural automation.

FellowAI is a company working to create automation in supply chain management and inventory optimization using artificial intelligence, computer vision, micro-asset positioning, and sensor fusion. In warehouses, this means AI, robotics, and machine learning work together to map layouts, manage space, and locate inventory, making the process faster and more precise.

Cobalt Robotics is in the security space, building autonomous robots that integrate with customer security operations to make workplaces more safe, secure, and productive. Their robots follow a mapped route and patrol spaces looking for unusual things like an open door, loud noises, spills, or a person where they are not supposed to be and use live video chat and video and audio sensors to assess situations and take any necessary actions.

Greensight uses autonomous drone hardware and sensors for aerial remote sensing and mapping to capture data and make smart choices using data analysis software. Greensight created a multispectral camera to capture five times the data of a regular camera. Their drones are used for land management and smart agriculture, bridge inspections, construction planning, and even monitoring the flow of traffic in a given area.

These are just a few examples of emerging tech industries and marketing in a world of evolving technology and new demands as a result of pursuing the self-driving moonshot. The push for autonomous vehicles is not relegated to cars alone.

What To Look For As An Investor

If you are looking into emerging technology markets from the perspective of an investor, there are certain indicators to watch out for.

Look for new technologies being proven in the space, including successful testing and whether or not the company is a developing brand or a mature company producing innovative tech. Each has different risks associated with them. A developing brand is valued mostly on their potential for sales, not profit, especially as they build out capacity and develop a new market for their products or services. Mature brands are valued more traditionally, by their profits, revenue growth, and sales.

Some questions to ask yourself when looking for investment opportunities include:
- What roles are the leading companies hiring for?
- Where did the new technology company come from?
- Is the founding team coming from a leading self-driving car tech company?
- Is the company pulling talent from other leading companies?
- What companies are self-driving car companies partnering with or acquiring?

You can also attend events in the autonomous vehicle space to network and gain new insights into emerging companies and technologies. The more educated you are about the space, the better you'll feel about making a smart choice. Nonetheless, investing in technology comes with risks.

Right now, the four highest-level and major drivers in the self-driving car space which fundamentally changes how the autonomous vehicles work are:
- Sensors. What they do and how they work are constantly evolving and are required for autonomous vehicles to 'see' the world around them.
- Computational power. This is rapidly and constantly evolving and the amount of power shifts how much an autonomous vehicle can do and for how long.

- Energy density. As batteries get denser and more energy-efficient, it pushes how far you can go and how much an autonomous vehicle can do on a single charge.
- Algorithms. Algorithms are always changing and being improved and every change has the potential to push the industry forward or in a new direction and improve capabilities.

These specific elements are directly moving the autonomous vehicle industry forward, so getting involved in any of these may be a good option for investors.

What Students Should Be Studying to be Marketable in the Emerging Tech Space

The technology space is dynamic and constantly evolving, and as new technology is invented and proven, the people companies hire and the skills they look for evolve, too. What companies were hiring for 10 years ago is different than what these new technology companies are hiring for now.

But it can be difficult or even impossible to study exactly what technology companies are looking for in new employees. Many companies have solved this by looking for the fundamentals. As a student, be sure to learn fundamental technologies and concepts like electrical engineering, computer science, and the core skills applicable in your desired field.

Once you fully understand the fundamentals and basics, many companies will hire you based on your potential and ability to learn the specific expertise needed to do the job. You can still study and practice things like perception systems, machine learning, and artificial intelligence, of course, but it is important to remember that these fields move forward and change so quickly that what you learn in school today may not be directly applicable in five years. This is why it is important to focus on core expertise and fundamentals before leveraging those skills to expand your capabilities on the job.

Omnitron Sensors

We are in an exciting age of technology, especially in the push to enable autonomous vehicles. It is truly the moonshot of our generation and there are so much innovation and creativity occurring in the space.

My company, Omnitron, saw a need for building robust, lower-cost, and higher-performing scanners for the LIDAR market and we created a whole new silicon photonics process. It is amazing to see the technology emerging from the original idea of a self-driving car.

I always had a passion for math and understanding how things work. I remember tinkering with and breaking a number of my dad's electronics to discover how they worked and why. I knew I wanted to learn more but wasn't sure what that would mean for a career. In college, I used math to build and create things, which led me to electrical engineering.

Being able to use math and imagination to innovate and take inspiration from the world around me and nature to apply concepts to technology to solve problems has been an amazing career and I am excited to see how the self-driving car revolution continues to expand our abilities and innovate technology in ways we cannot even imagine right now.

CHAPTER 7

FINDING YOUR NORTH STAR: HOW I GUIDED 14 COMPANIES TO PROFITABLE EXITS IN 15 YEARS

By **GREGORY SHEPARD**

Would you ever get in your car and just start driving to an unfamiliar destination with no directions or GPS? What if you are heading in the wrong direction? What if your route could be shorter and more direct?

Ironically, this is how most entrepreneurs and investors behave today. As companies evolve in their maturity, poor planning and lack of preparation are often exposed. In fact, nearly 90% of all startups fail before ever reaching scale. In my experience, this is due in large part to startups lacking what I call a North Star.

The North Star is designed to align a company to its end goal, including their potential acquirers, and sets the stage for its strategic vision. It acts as a GPS for your company, allowing you to begin with the end in mind and ensure the decisions made today are enabling the shortest and most direct route to your profitable exit in the future.

There are five strategic components of the North Star:
1. What

2. Why
3. Who
4. How Much
5. When

In this chapter, I will cover each element of a North Star and explain how you can leverage this process to drive your company toward a profitable exit.

But before I jump into that, I want to share a bit of my background with you.

About Me

I have built and sold 12 businesses in the last 15 years. During that time, I was the recipient of four private equity awards for transactions between $250M to $1B. Over those 15 years, I refined a methodology I call BOSS, the Business Operating Support System. It is this process that has led me to a 100% success rate in my investments. Today, I am the CEO and founding partner of BOSS Capital Partners, an investment firm focused on series seed technology businesses that prefer operational expertise and guidance to achieve capital-efficient and rewarding outcomes.

Whether it's a company I've built or one I'm investing in, I always start with the North Star.

The What

What does your company do? What does your product do? Although they seem similar, these are not the same questions. Often, startups have a difficult time defining what exactly they do for their customers, and they confuse what they do as a company with what problem their product or solution solves.

Let's look at the company side first. Your company is more than just a product or service; it is a culture, an ideology, and a feeling. It is important that you can explicitly describe exactly what value your company provides to the market. When developing your company "what" statement, focus on three things:

1. Description
2. Features
3. Benefits

First, the description, defined as a clear and concise explanation of your company. For the description, I like to focus on the meaning of your company. Guy Kawasaki, marketing expert, author, and venture capitalist, says that great companies are built around one of three meanings:

1. **Increasing the quality of life.** Your company makes people more productive or makes their lives easier or more enjoyable.
2. **Righting a wrong.** A variant on the above. Your organization is a part of the solution, not a part of the problem.
3. **Preventing the end of something good.** Your enterprise is working to preserve something classic or historical.

Notice how none of the options include making money and getting rich. That's on purpose. Consumers are savvier than ever and can spot insincerity from a mile away. If your meaning is not beneficial or does not connect emotionally to the customer, they will not engage.

The second focus of your description is determining your features. In order to carry out your meaning, as defined above, what features will you offer to your customers and the market? For instance, if your meaning is geared toward improving the quality of life, then your feature could potentially be offering 24/7 customer support, free services, price matching, etc. Keep in mind that these are your company's features, not the features of your product or service.

And lastly, you want to determine your company's benefits. Again, following the example, if the company's meaning is to increase the quality of life, and one of my features is 24/7 support, the benefits this provides my customers are peace of mind and job security.

Now, let's look at the what statement for your product. Using the same approach as above, you want to apply the same three steps to your product or service to determine its description, features, and benefits.

What you have now are two distinct what statements and the first element of the North Star.

The Why

The most valuable word in the human language is "why." In this case, why should the market choose to solve their problems with your solution? I break this section down into three parts;

1. **Problem**
2. **Solution**
3. **Impact**

The first step in compelling your customers and prospects to purchase your product or service is to accurately describe their problem.

The problem could be rooted in the status quo, or it may be a new or unforeseen problem. At any rate, you must prove to your customers and prospects that you understand what pains them the most or the biggest issues they face.

Once you have the problem identified, you need to accurately and completely describe your solution to that problem. Make sure as you describe your solution so that it is written in the voice of your customer. In many cases, we try to describe our solution from an inward-out perspective. It is always important to embody the customer's voice when describing your solution to ensure it resonates with your audience.

Finally, the last step in defining your why statement is to describe the impact your solution has on your customers. When describing the impact, do your best to use financial metrics positively impacted by your solution.

The Who

The "who" section of the North Star is split into two sections; the Ideal Customer Profile or ICP and the Ideal Acquirer Profile or IAP. This "who" is also the first step in developing your exit strategy. It is not by coincidence that the ICP and IAP are completed together. In fact, it is critical that your potential acquirers have the same ICP as you, as this ensures target market alignment and a smoother acquisition.

Ideal Customer Profile

In essence, an ideal customer profile is a description of the company, not the individual buyer or end-user, that is a perfect fit for your offering. In developing your ICP, you will be looking at company revenue, company size, and the number of employees, industry, vertical, size of customer base, technology in use, geography, ownership, customers, and products sold.

The first step in developing your ICP is to examine the existing customers who have found your offering to be a perfect solution to their problem. If you don't yet have customers, take a look at your closest competitors and the companies that have adopted their solution. Next, you will examine each of the above criteria for these customers.

What you are driving toward here is a series of straightforward statements that get to the heart of who your company should be talking to, which market segments to focus on and, in addition, addresses the customer needs - which can then be fulfilled by your offering. It addresses the who, but also the what and why that you developed earlier in the North Star phase of BOSS. These statements are easily assimilated into your go-to-market strategy.

Ideal Acquirer Profile

The development of your ideal acquirer profile (IAP) will focus on creating a clear and concise profile of who your potential acquirers are. This is a critical step in developing an exit strategy and designing your go-to-market approach. Remember the GPS analogy I mentioned earlier. From this point forward, you are plotting your destination and creating your turn-by-turn directions.

Making an IAP will require you to do some research into your industry's recent M&A activity. The first step is to identify the five most recent acquisitions in your space. Next, document how much each company was sold for and who they were sold to. Now take it a step further and identify the multiple each company was sold for and if it was based on top-line or bottom-line revenue.

Here is an example of the data you need to collect:
- Industry: Medical Imaging
- Acquisition Amount Average: $150M
- Top-line or Bottom-line: Top-line
- Average Multiple: 8X

Now that you have a list of the most recent acquirers and the deal characteristics, it is time to build your ideal acquirer profile.

Here are the profile data points:
- Industry
- What is their cash balance?
- What is their company size (Employees)?
- What is their company size (Revenue)?
- How many customers do they have?
- Who are their competitors?
- What are their needs?

With your IAP established, you can now move onto the final elements of the North Star.

The How Much & When

This is where the rubber meets the road. You are now in a position to have your vision and strategy validating reality. Most entrepreneurs enjoy this section the most, because who doesn't want to talk about when you sell and how much money you want to make, right?

Let's start with how much you can sell your startup for. Firstly, you will have to determine why the buyer wants to make an acquisition; it is typically either to save money or make money. Both are viable, however, in today's economic climate, companies who can help their buyers save money are being acquired at a premium.

Second, you will look at what the buyer hopes to acquire. Are they more interested in acquiring the intellectual property and/or the resident knowledge and expertise of the executive team? Or is the buyer more interested in how your product can benefit their company?

Third, you'll take a look at the buyer's viewpoint on top-line revenue versus bottom-line revenue. You'll need to know which one is most important to the buyer and, as well, which one your startup is best at contributing to.

Fourth, you'll look at the drivers that motivate the buyer. There are four elements here: revenue growth (actual and percentage growth year over year), retention rate (customers retained from one period to another), profit margin (how many cents of profit a business has generated for each dollar of sale), and base and attachment rate.

Fifth, you'll need to explore the top-line and bottom-line multiples the buyer has in mind and apply them to your top-line and bottom-line revenue to arrive at a sale price.

Regarding when you can sell, there are three things to look at:
1. Revenue
2. Profitability
3. Exit Metrics

Revenue encompasses a working product with paying clients and product validation. Profitability encompasses expense, income, and profit, and determines your break-even point. Exit metrics encompass the achievement of the metrics you worked toward when determining how much you can sell for (growth, retention, margin, and attachment rate). Goals are established for each of these categories. They are then plotted on a chart. When the end goals have been reached, you are ready to sell!

Summary

"Begin with the end in mind means to begin each day, task, or project with a clear vision of your desired direction and destination, and then continue by flexing your proactive muscles to make things happen." – Stephan Covey, educator, speaker, and author of *The 7 Habits of Highly Effective People*.

This is the concept behind the BOSS North Star.

By beginning with the end in mind, i.e., determining who your ideal buyers are before you build the company, you gain a strategic advantage that drastically reduces the time to exit. Not only does this ensure you have the right mission, vision, and key objectives to build the company around, but it also aligns your ICP with your eventual acquirers ICP, ultimately making your company extremely attractive to potential buyers. By aligning your ICP with your business roadmap, you will burn less cash while achieving your growth milestones, resulting in less dilution for you and your team.

The BOSS methodology and framework perfectly blends strategy and execution to give you specific steps from day one to achieve your growth targets and key objectives.

CHAPTER 8

CRISIS MARKETING: HOW TO SURVIVE AND THRIVE DURING RECESSIONS, PANDEMICS, AND BUBBLE BURSTS

By J.C. GRANGER

Marketing in a time of crisis is like no other type of marketing. Under normal circumstances, marketing strategies focus on infrastructure and long-term impact; marketing is usually about sustainability and growth.

During a crisis, these foundational marketing strategies don't apply. During a crisis, survival is the priority.

Think of it as if you accidentally got lost in the woods and the temperature dropped to zero overnight. Your body is going to say "Listen, John, I know you love playing the piano but the fingers have to go." When you're freezing, your body cuts off blood to the extremities and prioritizes the core organs to increase your chances of survival. And when something drastic happens, you have to do the same thing with your company.

Unfortunately for many companies, they put their marketing efforts in the same category as their fingers and don't realize that marketing is really more like their lungs. You can go without oxygen for a couple of minutes maybe, but go too long without it, and eventually, you'll die.

If you slash your marketing budget because you're trying to cut costs, your company will most likely be dead in 90 days regardless. It's a sad reality, but a reality all the same.

Think about it like this: A dry pipeline is a slow killer, regardless of external factors (the crisis) you're experiencing. Your company must have clients and money coming in to keep going.

Henry Ford, the founder of Ford Motor Company, once said, "A man who stops advertising to save money is like a man who stops a clock to save time."

Don't stop the clock, ever.

If your company is going to stay alive and even thrive, you must preserve your marketing budget during a crisis. Instead of cutting marketing, you're going to have to make sacrifices elsewhere. They're not fun to make, but they'll keep you alive.

Try Using a Marketing Agency

Consider the idea that cutting marketing staff might be a good option for you. Internal full-time marketing staff costs a considerable amount of money - money you could redirect to your marketing efforts.

You might have someone on staff who you're paying $50,000 a year. In reality, they cost you about $65,000 per year due to soft costs like benefits, payroll taxes, and paid time off.

During a crisis, think about how far $65,000 in a paid ad budget will go over a year.

The answer is far.

If possible, you want to keep your top marketing strategist on staff because they will help guide your company through the crisis. However, you will most likely have to cut other internal staff to save money.

From there, consider outsourcing your marketing to a marketing agency. They're significantly less expensive and often have more bandwidth and expertise. Additionally, these agencies often pay for the expensive marketing software needed for successful campaigns, which also saves your company money.

Whereas your internal marketing staff might be experts in a specific area, marketing agencies have a larger staff with a broader area of expertise. It's quite possible that agency experts will unlock a side to marketing that your business has never taken advantage of before.

With marketing agencies, you get more experienced marketing personnel for less money. It's a win-win, especially when you consider the money you can redirect to your overall marketing budget.

While no one likes laying off staff, it is important during a time of crisis to think more big-picture and make hard decisions for the ultimate health and survival of the overall business.

Reprioritize Marketing Efforts During a Crisis

During a crisis, you must reprioritize your marketing strategy. If a component of your strategy doesn't provide you with an immediate short-term lead generation response, cut it.

Think about this:

Search Engine Optimization (SEO) is a long-term strategy. Companies that successfully integrate SEO can generate between 50%-80% of their revenue from organic searches. Maybe, before the crisis, your marketing team sought to develop a valuable SEO pipeline.

That being said, if you're not already making a ton of money from your existing SEO strategy, then cut it for the time being. During a crisis, short-term ROI strategies must be prioritized over the long-term ones. It's all about what is going to work right now and not the things that may pay off months down the road.

Organic social media is excellent for long-term branding. But during a crisis, when in the long-run your business could be non-existent, organic social media just isn't as valuable.

However, you SHOULD keep social media paid ads because those can deliver a quick, short-term lead turnaround. But nix the purely organic posts as those will have little to no reach or short-term impact.

The only exception to this is if your company or product can't do paid social media advertising. You must keep up organic social efforts and prioritize other quick turnaround marketing if you're in a restricted industry, like cannabis for example.

What else should you cut?

Written content. As much as it hurts my marketing soul to say this, during a crisis, how-to guides, white papers, and blog posts aren't worth your time, energy, or money.

Unless your business is to make money writing content (like a blogger or publisher), cut written content. Simply put, if it isn't generating significant ROI, you have to get rid of it for now.

Lastly, public relations (PR) has to go. During a crisis, no one cares about your press releases or seeing you on TV. These marketing efforts cost a lot of time and money, and there's no audience for them during uncertain times.

In the long term, SEO, social media, content, and PR are all valuable parts of a successful marketing strategy, but during uncertain times, these measures aren't a priority.

Remember, you don't have to get rid of these marketing strategies permanently. These are temporary changes that will help your company survive the crisis and outlast the competition.

Again, the goal here is to stay alive. Survive the cold night and live to tell the story.

What Marketing Strategies Should You Concentrate On?

During a crisis, here are the main marketing verticals you should focus on:

- PPC (Pay-per-click) ads
- Email marketing
- Text message marketing (for B2C consumer products)
- LinkedIn direct outreach (for B2B companies)

Pay-per-click Ads

When you create a paid advertising campaign and launch it, the results are immediate. Instantaneously, your ad starts appearing and people begin engaging and clicking on them in almost real-time. For immediate lead generation, paid ads generate clicks, which is why this is a marketing priority.

I remember a software client we had a couple of years back. They were a B2B SaaS (software as a service) company and they had pretty ambitious goals. They were in a tight spot because they came to us already on their last leg of marketing budget and needed a Hail Mary miracle campaign ASAP and to be profitable "yesterday" so to speak.

Now, normally I don't touch situations like that with a 10-foot pole because it's typically a recipe for disappointment because PPC campaigns take time to optimize. That being said, I'm a complete geek for B2B software and I knew their only real chance was a successful PPC campaign for quick results.

Now, "quick results" can go in either direction. Sometimes they are simply bad results quickly. If you create a low-converting campaign and turn it on, you can blow through thousands of dollars almost overnight if you're not careful. However, if you know what you're doing or you hire someone who does and create a high-converting campaign, you can absolutely crush it almost overnight as well.

Luckily, that was the outcome for our software client and we were able to get them amazing results in a short amount of time. They ended up doubling down on that success and it helped them turn the corner to get back on track with all of their marketing and year-end growth goals.

The moral of the story is PPC is a fast-results marketing vertical and if you're in a bind, a high-converting campaign can turn things around fast.

Email Marketing

Email is also an effective way of marketing. Think about it: email marketing is accessible - nearly everyone has email access on their computers and smartphones. With email marketing, turnaround and activity are immediate. People get an email and a good percentage of them will immediately open, click, and/or reply.

Another thing to remember is email is the ORIGINAL form of marketing. Back in the late 90s, there was no PPC, SEO, social media, or text message marketing. Email was pretty much it from a digital standpoint.

I "cut my teeth," so to speak, on email marketing back in the early 2000s. It was my first real dive into digital marketing. And I went all in. I actually learned about email marketing from a bulk email marketer.

Most would probably refer to him as a "spammer," because he absolutely was. I didn't like the "shotgun" approach to bulk emailing, but I was fascinated with how the process worked and why bulk marketers operated the way they did.

One thing I learned that I still use to this day is how insanely important analytics is for email marketing. Bulk marketers live and die by the stats. If they're running a campaign to a million email addresses, they watch the stats like a hawk, looking for any sharp drops in open or click-through rates. If they see that, then they shut down their campaign immediately. Why? Because that's their cue that the Internet Service Providers (ISPs) or Email Service Providers (ESPs) have caught on to them and are moving their emails to people's spam box automatically.

I took the lessons of email analytics with me in my digital marketing career but adapted them to my own email marketing style, which was more a "sniper" than "shotgun" approach. Military snipers have a saying: "One shot. One kill." It's a testament to their style of learning as much about their target as possible and being patient. Then only when the timing and situation give them the best chance at success do they take their shot.

When dealing with a crisis that is affecting your business, it can be extremely tempting to take a "shotgun" approach and just hope by throwing every strategy and resource at the problem, something will stick. Resist this temptation at all costs. When you're in survival mode, you can't afford to waste a single dollar on a strategy that isn't laser-focused and optimized to convert into the most ROI possible.

Text Message Marketing

Like emails, most people are checking their text messages many times each day. Text message marketing can be effective if you offer consumer products. Daily deals and coupons offered via text message perform well and can typically generate almost immediate sales. One statistic you may be surprised to see is that text message marketing has an extremely high read rate - 97% - within 15 minutes of users receiving the text.

One of the most successful text message campaigns I've ever conducted was for restaurants and bars in downtown Denver. It was insanely easy. We would text food and drink specials for their slowest days to patrons who had already been to their establishments or those who lived in proximity to them. People would show up and show the text to redeem the deal.

The restaurants and bars were happy because they would get almost immediate turnaround business for their slowest days and the patrons were happy because they would get a great deal on a day they normally wouldn't get discounts. They would even forward the text to their friends so the restaurants and bars wouldn't just get the people on their list coming in. They would get 3-8 people for every one person who came in from their marketing list. And if you have an e-commerce website, this tactic is effective in a very similar way.

Using texts for marketing is very cost-effective and improves mobile engagement, which many businesses are looking for, especially in a crisis. The reason it is so cost-effective is that the only costs associated with text marketing is the cost of a text messaging service to deliver your messages. My personal favorite is www.tatango.com.

LinkedIn Direct Outreach

If you're a B2B company, consider starting LinkedIn outreach during a crisis. For example, you could hire an agency or purchase software to begin automated LinkedIn outreach for your business. As long as you develop a strong targeting and messaging strategy, you will get direct responses from a very engaged professional audience of decision-makers.

If you upgrade your LinkedIn to a paid premium subscription, you can more specifically target profitable prospects using industry, job title, location, years of experience, and company size parameters. Build a list of viable contacts and begin your outreach efforts.

For B2B companies, this has an immediate lead generation return. The most effective method for LinkedIn outreach is to automate half of the process, which makes it scalable when leads begin funneling in. The other half of the process is very manual because you really do need to build a genuine relationship, but it's a very powerful form of marketing when done correctly.

If you do decide to automate part of the process, there are a ton of tools out there that can help you with this. The one I like the most right now is GrowthLead.io. They are priced fairly, cloud-based, and have a great user interface along with good customer service.

Just Remember...

No company wants to have to consider what steps they'd have to take during a crisis. But unfortunately, crises don't care if you've prepared or not and they can come in many forms such as recessions, pandemics, and bubble bursts. They strike without warning and they can tank your company in a heartbeat if you don't know how to respond.

The fact is that crisis marketing is like no other kind of marketing. So, to ensure your company's survival, you must learn how to properly navigate the chaos, and it all begins with reprioritizing (not cutting) your marketing budget and strategy to focus on immediate short-term results. Once the recession, pandemic, bubble burst, or other crisis has passed, your company will be able to once again restrategize and look toward long-term results.

My company, Infinity Marketing Group, has helped hundreds of companies survive past crisis situations and are currently working with businesses to continue to grow during the COVID-19 pandemic. You can reach out to us anytime for advice and support of your business and thrive even during a time of chaos.

Email us at Info@InfinityMgroup.com or visit our website at www.InfinityMgroup.com.

CHAPTER 9

COMMERCIALIZATION OF DISRUPTIVE MEDICAL TECHNOLOGY

By **JOSEPH C. MCGINLEY. M.D., PH.D.**

It's easy to know when a new medication is on the market. We've all seen a million commercials telling us to "ask your doctor if _____ is right for you!"

Every time a new and disruptive technology is invented or improved upon, it's splashed all over the news, featured in bright, colorful TV commercials, and getting reviewed on YouTube. Cars with collision assist, TVs with improved screen quality, phones with new camera settings...

You always know your options, right?

When it comes to commercially available products, yes. When it comes to disruptive medical technology? Not so much.

Medical technology entrepreneurship is a very different and frustrating process compared to the commercialization of traditional products and even medications. The patients don't know the product exists - and in most cases, neither do their doctors.

In almost every industry, the general steps are the same: create a product concept, secure funding, prototype/test the product, and finally institute sales.

In the medical tech field, the process of commercializing a product differs from other industries in that it first needs to pass regulatory compliance reviews with the FDA, then support and buy-in from physicians, before finally, the purchasing process - which is typically not run by physicians.

All of that happens without patients even being aware of the development and production of a technology that could significantly improve safety, reduce the cost of procedures, expedite recovery time, and more.

The main issue lies in purchasing. I hope the insights I have gained will help others navigate this challenging hurdle in the system.

IntelliSense® HandHeld Robotic Drill

The IntelliSense Drill Technology® may sound simple at first. However, it's an orthopedic power drill with patented, advanced, integrated sensor technology. Many people probably assume surgical drills are more advanced than the ones found in their garages. They are not, not until IntelliSense®.

Traditionally, if you have a broken bone that needs a plate and screws attached, this is the process: First, the surgeon opens the tissue, visualizes the broken bone and uses their hands to realign it, places the plate on one side of the bone, then uses a drill to bore a hole through the bone to the other side, then sets the drill down and picks up a measuring device (essentially a ruler) to determine the screw size, after which they place the screw to hold the plate in place.

IntelliSense Drill Technology® improves that entire process through the use of integrated sensors.

In contrast to IntelliSense® devices, most orthopedic power tools currently in use lack sensors, software, and real-time monitoring. Existing orthopedic tools and surgical practices require surgeons to rely on "feel" to determine if a drill they are using goes too far into or through the bone they are seeking to repair. Drilling too far or through a bone can seriously damage a patient's blood vessels, nerves, tendons, and other structures and organs. This problem known as "plunging" in the medical profession is a common risk in orthopedic surgeries. In addition to surgical errors caused by plunging, most orthopedic surgeons rely on manual measurement devices to determine the length of fixation screws. These devices are inaccurate and time-consuming to use. Misplaced screws result in extended time in the operating room (OR) and possibly additional surgeries to fix. Screws that are too short may fail to hold and require revision surgeries; screws that extend too far through a bone can damage adjacent blood vessels, nerves, and tendons and cause injury or even death.

Current procedures for avoiding such surgical errors require orthopedic surgeons to stop their work repeatedly to manually measure and re-measure drilling depths and screw lengths. Intraoperative x-rays (fluoroscopy) are often obtained to confirm satisfactory screw sizing and placement. These interruptions in the surgical process are very costly. They create a risk of additional errors and infection. They consume the expensive time of operating rooms and surgical teams. Moreover, they expose patients and medical staff to damaging radiation. Globally, preventable orthopedic surgical errors cost in excess of $1.5 billion per year. This cost falls on patients, healthcare providers, and health insurers. The sensors, software, and real-time monitoring and measurement capabilities of IntelliSense® products can dramatically reduce orthopedic surgical errors, waste, and their associated economic costs.

Medical literature says that up to 24% of orthopedic screws are placed incorrectly. Twenty-four percent! Patients are unaware when going into surgery and there is no set standard in medicine for performing this procedure accurately.

Imagine if the auto industry allowed up to 24% of screws to be incorrect sizes or placed in the wrong location when assembling cars!

The IntelliSense® Drill is a pretty simple to understand technology that is truly disruptive and innovative for the medical field and saves time and money while improving safety.

Yet, the product is continuously running into roadblocks within the purchasing process.

The Purchasing Process

Once the medical tech product has passed all levels of regulatory compliance, and there are doctors interested in using it, those doctors go to their administrators in the purchasing departments and ask them to bring in the technology. IntelliSense Drill Technology® does not lack in surgeon champions. Many leaders in the field want to use the technology but struggle to get the systems they work in to adopt it. The technology never gets past the admin purchasing process.

There are three main barriers to entry in the admin purchasing process: not recognizing the benefit of the product, maintaining the status quo, and established relationships with vendors.

The admins are typically not clinicians, so they may not be able to immediately see the **benefit of a new product**. Using the IntelliSense® Drill as an example, it is objectively better for both the surgeons and the patients compared to the traditional bone drill and depth gauge. However, when an admin sees the order for a new, potentially expensive product, their first question is going to be, "Why do you need this if you already have a drill and depth gauge?"

On top of not seeing the immediate benefit, hospital and practice administrators typically want to **stick to the status quo.** Right now, if one of their doctors needs a new drill, the admin only needs to go into the system, select the quantity, and click "order."

Setting up a new vendor can be a time-consuming task. There is the information-gathering stage, submitting and passing the Approval Committee, Purchasing Committee, and Use Committee. Then it needs to be entered into their system and updates need to be made to the use cards for all of the surgeons. Moreover, they need to create space to store the new equipment, figure out and assign a maintenance schedule, and keep track of reordering. They also need to train the operating room and sterilization staff on how to use, store, and sterilize the new product.

The amount of time and effort it takes to actually purchase and use a new device in a hospital is often a significant barrier to entry for most new technology in the medical field.

The other big issue is the **existing vendor relationships.** If a hospital has used the same bone drill vendor for many years, they know the reps and have built trust and a relationship over time. If an admin calls the long-term vendor to say they are going in another direction, that vendor rep will do everything in their power to keep their client. They will argue for the hospital to stick with them and remind them how much work it is to push new products out. Who will the admin want to listen to - the new guy or the rep they've known for years?

Creating a new product is not the challenge. The challenge is getting it into the doctor's hands. In one instance, a surgeon attended eight meetings advocating for IntelliSense® because he knew it was better for his patients - only to be told the administration was not willing to upset a large industry leader/vendor. Patients are unaware they are not getting the latest technologies or that the possibility of a higher standard of care is available.

In the end, if a product is better for patients and doctors, if the device is safer and more cost-effective, hospitals and practices should adopt it. Ideally, there would be no barrier to entry and the best product would always be put in place, but processes impede that scenario.

In many cases, large hospitals are prioritizing upfront costs over long-term savings and improved patient care - even when they don't realize it. Unfortunately, the patient care team does not work closely with the purchasing admins, each in their own silo in the system. This creates an unintentional lack of communication. This is common in large systems where it is harder to communicate. Because the purchasing team members are typically not part of the care team for patients, they are not seeing the nuances or benefits to either the physicians or the patients.

Other Amazing Medical Tech

IntelliSense® Drill is far from the only disruptive medical technology to run into the brick wall of commercialization. There are other revolutionary products changing the way medicine is performed.

Sonex Health is a great example. The Sonex SX-One MicroKnife facilitates carpal tunnel release using ultrasound guidance. Traditionally, carpal tunnel surgery is an open surgery, meaning there is an open incision at the base of the palm of the hand, and then they cut the transverse carpal ligament to release pressure on the median nerve. They close the skin with stitches, which need to be removed in the doctor's office one to two weeks later. The recovery time is typically 6-8 weeks.

Sonex's product utilizes ultrasound guidance, is minimally invasive (not an open surgery), and only needs lidocaine for numbing. No general anesthesia is needed and the incision is so small it does not require stitches. Most patients return to work in 48 hours. It's objectively better than open surgery with a very high success rate, low risk of complications, and much faster recovery.

Yet, acceptance is slower than I would expect. Many medical professionals are reluctant to change. It is the old adage: If something works, why fix it? This is despite the new approach being a simpler procedure, with drastically reduced recovery times.

Another simple yet elegant example is Siemens Medical Imaging ACUSON Freestyle™ Ultrasound. Siemens was the first company to widely commercialize a wireless ultrasound system. With traditional ultrasound machines, the probe has a cord directly tethered to the monitor. The Siemens ACUSON Freestyle™ has a wireless probe. This may not sound like a big deal, but when a physician is doing a procedure, they have a limited sterile field. Dragging a corded probe from one side of the body to the other can be a challenge. The wireless probes make it easy to move and still remain in the sterile field at all times. The cordless version allows for optimal physician positioning. This technology was introduced to the market almost a decade ago and is still not standard across the medical field.

In response to a need I saw in my own practice, McGinley Orthopedics, in collaboration with other partners, developed an augmented reality headset that works with any ultrasound machine. This system eliminates the need for a monitor. With the McGinley AR for Ultrasound system and the wireless probe, not only can I stay completely contained in the sterile field, but the ultrasound image is projected in my field of view making it so I do not have to turn my head away from the patient to see the screen. This is particularly useful when doing precise procedures like stem cells and platelet-rich plasma (PRP). I can see the injection site simultaneously with the ultrasound image. Yet another way technology is advancing treatments and improving care.

How to Navigate the Purchasing Problem?

That's the big question! It is one we are still answering.

With new companies, their biggest advantages are flexibility, adaptability, and creativity. Large established companies can't change on a dime or pivot to new directions as easily. New companies are nimble and have the ability to respond to physician feedback and redesign for better patient outcomes. While smaller size allows for flexibility, new innovative companies don't have the market infiltration to easily influence change.

Part of the challenge is messaging. Small companies with new technologies need to communicate benefits both to the purchasing teams AND to patients directly. In this age of information and social media, we can effectively reach patients directly - the consumers - in the same way pharmaceutical companies began doing decades ago.

We created a website and portal (myorthostory.com) where patients can share their stories of problems and issues with orthopedic plate and screw surgeries. Here they can see they are not alone. We give information directly to consumers and teach them to advocate for themselves. While it is common for patients to ask their doctor about a new drug they think might be relevant to them, patients don't typically ask about what tools and technology surgeons are using prior to surgery. We are trying to bring patients' voices to the table. Asking those questions of surgeons brings needed awareness so they can become advocates as well.

We are employing multiple other strategies. We created videos of doctors using and discussing the IntelliSense® Drill and we bring those and the patient experiences to hospital administrators to talk to them about the product. We work with commercial insurers to promote reimbursement to use better technology, stating the evidence shows it will save them money while providing patients with improved care. We talk to insurers about how our product decreases the need for repeat/corrective surgeries, reduces operating room time and cost as well as reduces waste. We show them that we can be part of the greater solution. If the product can be reimbursed through insurers it will, in turn, help the purchasing admin see the benefit of change.

We also participate in a community called OrthoFounders, made up of orthopedic surgeons who started their own companies to fill a need in the medical field. It's a great place to share information, discuss strategies, and help each other.

We still do traditional marketing and sales and go to trade shows, of course. It's all a learning process and we continue to learn, grow, and pivot as needed. We are lucky to have so many surgeons championing our product and willing to assist in our efforts.

Patients have been a great source of information for my practice and medical device company. Often, they have spent countless hours researching their specific issue. I never discount their findings or experiences. Many have told me about or introduced me to technology and procedures I didn't know existed. If it proves to be good for my patients, I incorporate them into my practice.

To all readers and patients:
Do your research. Be your own best advocate. Ask questions and keep asking until you get the answers you need.

To healthcare providers:
The practice of medicine has never seen such rapid advancement. It is time we embrace new technologies to ensure better outcomes for our patients. The tech in combination with our collective talents can help to solve the problems our healthcare system faces.

As physicians, we do our best to provide the greatest care to our patients but we need the patients, administrators, and insurers to support us. It is a team effort! I am proud to play my part.

CHAPTER 10

BUILDING A GLOBAL STAFF

By **KURT SNYDER**

There are many advantages to a U.S. business developing and nurturing a dedicated business team made up of professionals dispersed throughout the world. Leveraging an international staff of sub-contractors allows an agile and flexible domestic firm to lower labor costs, make shifts from fixed to variable overhead, and mitigate the risks inherent in a geographical concentration of staff which may be negatively impacted by political events and/or natural disasters.

Building this human capital asset would have been nearly impossible only 15 years ago. The advent of real-time communication technologies and robust hiring platforms has brought the world of professional talent right to the doorstep of savvy firms seeking the benefits of offshore human resources. Never before in history has it been so easy for a firm in Chicago to find, engage, and hire a freelancer 8000 miles and 14 time zones away in Bangladesh and be transacting business in a matter of hours. Platforms such as Linkedin, Indeed, Upwork, and Fiverr, in combination with Skype for Business, Zoom, Slack, and ClickUp have made it a reality to quickly integrate offshore teams into domestic business practices. Many businesses today might have staff working on four or five continents and with 12-hour time differences.

It may sound easy to build a global team. I can assure you, it is not. Just ask the United Nations. There is a side to this endeavor that you will only hear from those who have attempted and sustained it. The process is fraught with challenges. It is highly time-consuming, labor-intensive, and at times, an emotional rollercoaster of victories and defeat. Over the past five years of building such a team, it has become as much an art as a science. The nitty-gritty grunt work of accessing the right talent pools from the right nations with the right work offers is not for the faint of heart.

The art of the process lies in the rigorous and disciplined approach toward recruiting, the trust which must be built to retain staff in the absence of physical proximity, and the necessary bridge forged to close the inherent gaps of communicating across vast expanses of time and distance. When these three functional operations are carried out in an organized and integrated manner, the synergies created will drive a marked multiplier effect upon business growth.

Accessing the Right Talent Pools & Recruitment

There are many factors to consider before embarking on a recruitment journey. These include having a clear sense of the skill set required for the role, how, or if, cultural or time factors might impact the delivery of work, and knowing what job platform to use. In many ways, it's really no different than the practice of hiring someone locally; however, the anticipated challenges of offshore staffing must be taken into account well before the recruitment process begins. A disciplined and methodical approach to this phase of global team building will almost always yield a great return on the time invested.

A great quote I once heard from a colleague went something like this: "Accessing gig workers on platforms such as Fivver and Upwork is like one big race to the bottom of the global talent and business ethics pool." It's doubtful anyone will be rushing to print that on a T-shirt any time soon. But while that can be true, it does not have to be. What we have found is that at times, someone who is an expert in his or her field can make much more money than if they sold their services to just one employer. We have often discovered that the true hyper-experts of digital marketing are so good that they choose not to allow any single firm to "own" them. Why limit yourself to finding a Facebook, Google, or email marketing expert within a reasonable commute to your office when you can access the entire world? If it sounds like we're making a coded argument against institutional monogamy… that's for you to decide.

We painstakingly post job roles across these platforms. As there is far more to this approach than merely "setting and forgetting" a post, it is imperative that you nurture and optimize the campaign, and remain patient, as it might take days, weeks, or months for a quality candidate to come in. The key is to also know that more traditional interviewing approaches may prove unsuccessful, as you will clearly not be meeting face to face. Learning the communications and professional branding habits of candidates on a pre-interview basis, conducting multiple video conference interviews, and doing a full web check are critical tasks in the decision-making process of whom to hire. It's sort of like deciding on a nanny without doing any vetting. It's just a recipe for having a Lifetime movie based on your story.

I cannot tell you how many candidates never make it to the first interview, merely due to what's revealed in their communications habits. Do they have Skype? If they don't, it's a red flag. Is their personal email domain something unprofessional such as mickeymouse25@gmail.com? Is their name written in all lower-case letters in the email? What does their Linkedin, Skype, or Twitter profile picture reveal? Do they send emails that could have come from straight from the texts of your 16-year-old daughter? Not to be ageist, but by that I mean, all-lowercase text, over-use of abbreviations, no punctuation, and emojis? Are their emails loaded with spelling errors, grammatical errors, or use of language styles that might signal challenges in the future? Going back and forth with a candidate in multiple ways across multiple apps can give you a preliminary picture of their overall business savvy, and whether there might be communication or cultural divides from the get-go.

Set a position interview time that is convenient for their part of the world. Then suddenly change it to midnight their time to see what reaction you get. They'll initially tell you that working North American hours is no issue at all, but then you'll soon see their true "work-day" habits emerge before it's too late. They'll tell you they are entirely plugged in during North American hours, but then you'll notice long lags of hours or even a day when responding back to a simple email or ping. We often give up on a candidate well before ever advancing them to a Zoom interview.

Video conference interviews are also an excellent method to glean a candidate's peripheral skills of tech-savviness and adaptiveness. Schedule a Zoom meeting for the first interview. Use JoinMe or WebEx for the second interview and see if the process runs equally as smoothly. If the candidate truly has worked successfully serving global employers, partners, and clients, the fluid use of these various video conferencing apps should be second nature. Using all of these secret evaluation methods will make you feel like an undercover intelligence officer.

When you launch and enter the interview room, of course, no differently than a job interview, they should be early and waiting to be admitted and should present themselves professionally. It speaks volumes to us when the candidate is at the conference 5 to 7 minutes before an actual call. Like my high school track coach used to say, "when you're early, you're on time." But if they're actually late? Forget it. Late with a tech issue excuse? Forget it. When the video connects, to what lengths did the candidate go to be on the cutting edge of a high-quality representation? Is the lighting good? Is the audio good? Do they use a green screen and a virtual background? Is the background neutral to anyone seeing it? If they do not use a virtual background, is there anything at all in their natural background that is distracting to the viewer? A weird poster? A screaming child? You'll know when you see it.

You might be thinking that all of this focus on communication details a bit over the top if I'm hiring an analyst or a bookkeeper. We are assessing a person's entire attitude and attention to detail with respect to their professional brand. If a candidate cannot address these basic items, then we already know they are not a fit for the perfectionist corporate culture we have at my firm. Furthermore, digital communications are the only way we'll be able to work effectively together and maximize synergy. Thus, if you are hiring globally, you must pay heed to these early warning signs of eventual issues.

Building Trust to Motivate & Retain Talent

It is challenging enough to engage, motivate, and provide career growth to a locally-based traditional staff of professionals. Add to that the time, space, and cultural nuances that come with offshore teams and you are in for a unique set of hurdles. Yet, people are people, no matter how far away they are or from what culture they derive.

The base-level human emotions of fear, greed, and vanity cut across nearly every culture, and so it's only a matter of accommodating this sameness via non-physically-present communications and policies which allow you to mold and sustain high-performing global teams. I've been told people have some good traits as well.

Having traveled the world, and being a simple man, I have come to the simple conclusion that people are people, no matter what country they live in, or what their religion or politics might be. We are all more the same than we are different. All employees from all cultures want to have security, predictability, and be recognized and rewarded for their efforts. Beyond that, they want to feel like they are part of a group and derive some meaning from the time they invest in a livelihood. It's important, however, to view and engage staff from a range of nations through their own cultural, political, and economic lenses and not to overlay an entirely American-centric viewpoint on the situations.

I've learned that many cultural stereotypes of a wide range of nations are not true. My firm seeks only ambitious, highly-motivated individuals who might just have an imbalance toward work and wealth creation over leisure in their personal work-life balance equation. Historically, the only way for young international professionals to tap into the prosperity and rewards of the U.S. capitalist free-market economy was to try to move here for a job. Today's world affords them the opportunity of having the best of both worlds. They can work for a U.S. firm that serves U.S. clients, but not have to dislocate from friends, family, and a culture they love. Also, due to the widespread corruption that pervades many fast-developing economies, working as a business owner for a client in the U.S. represents a way of bypassing much of the extortion and unsavory business practices of our employees' native countries.

Upon engaging a new staff member from across the globe, it's very important to fully grasp the economic realities he or she might be facing. A simple Google search of "average white-collar monthly salary" in the nation from which your candidate stems will give you a great idea of what your "competition" might be. As an example, we have engaged several young, highly-talented professionals from Ukraine. Ukraine saw its economy greatly recede after the 2014 Russian invasion of Crimea and, as a result, wages plummeted and job prospects became bleak. We have been able to pay some Ukrainian-based staff three times more than what they might otherwise make domestically, yet it still might be a salary three times less than what we would pay here in the U.S. for the same role. Like if your favorite food was salad, it's a true win-win. Both for us and our staffer and it also brings us great employee friend referrals, as we have earned the reputation of delivering great financial rewards for comparable work.

Over and above base-level income, we also offer profit-sharing via bonus pools to our international staff, as well as the opportunity to transition out of what amounts to "tech sweatshops" run by U.S. firms in these nations. Most have told us that it is entirely unprecedented in their experience to receive a bonus when working for North American or U.S. firms. We even have one staff member who left a prized position with the esteemed firm, Accenture, to come work with us. Working for us, she makes 300% more than she did working for Accenture, not to mention she no longer must commute for four hours round trip per day into a major city. To me, there is nothing more important to tapping the true excellence of a staff member, be it domestically or internationally, than to make him or her feel some degree of ownership of the financial value they may have created as well as to improve their working lifestyle.

Of course, money is not the only motivating factor in maintaining positive morale and a rock-solid work culture. There are several non-monetary elements of what an offshore employer can deliver which are equally as important. Maslow's hierarchy of needs, the social theory on what directs human behavior, purports that after basic survival and safety needs are met, humans then begin to prioritize belongingness and prestige. To the extent that an employer, domestic or offshore, can also deliver against the need for belongingness and camaraderie (no, that doesn't mean organizing Zoom happy hours, avoid that) and create a working environment that recognizes achievement and a feeling of accomplishment, it will highly increase its chances of building and sustaining morale.

To this end, we hold monthly all staff Zoom meetings where we not only report out results but we also recognize the individual efforts of our partners. During these sessions, we encourage presenters to discuss any non-business elements of their personal lives, country, or cultures which they are proud of and would like to share with the entire team. These sessions have become one of the favorite aspects of working together, as no one has yet come up with the virtual donut box in the kitchen, nor a virtual birthday cake.

Building trust and motivating a workforce are challenges every business faces. Add to that the challenge of connecting on a human level with a workforce spread across the world, and you face an even greater challenge. However, it can be done when employers adapt to the cultural and geographical contexts in which their staff work, or even perceive work. Just as money is not the only motivating factor in a domestic job, there are other lifestyle-related dimensions to the job that must be taken into account.

Overcoming Time & Distance in Streamlining Operations

When I reflect back ten years and recall the vast turbulence of trying to work with teams in Africa and the Caribbean Islands, it seems like three lifetimes ago when compared to today. Since the mid-2000s, quantum leaps have occurred in communications technology, which has fostered a historic opportunity to integrate teams as if they were literally in cubicles and offices right within your building. New and improved video conferencing platforms, real-time instant messaging, project management applications, and robust international payment software has brought the world of white-collar talent right to the doorstep of any U.S.-based firm.

Long before work from home became de rigueur for U.S. firms (and I'm talking pre-pandemic times), we were early adopters and masters of project management applications such as Skype, Zoom, Slack, and ClickUp. These applications were second nature to us long before it seemed many U.S. firms latched on and a lifetime before desperate corporations were forced to embrace them for survival in a new pandemic world. For us, it was not a matter of convenience, but one of pure necessity. By what other means would you have dozens of staff communicating and collaborating on real-time projects when they are spread thousands of miles apart and across a dozen time zones? Thank goodness we are not relegated to fax machines, international shipping, and email! We literally could not have molded this cohesive global work team without these platforms that seem to have only recently become noticed by most in business.

In fact, it was only when the entire world seemed to jump onto these platforms in a matter of a few weeks that pioneers like us began to feel the pain of tech issues that come with over-stressed platforms and data usage. Quality connectivity is now so central to our business model that we have had to invest in our staff's hardware and connectivity. Thank you for that, COVID.

When we first forayed into the use of offshore staff back in 2008, there was basically just one way to pay people, and that was with a primitive version of PayPal by today's standards. Since then, PayPal has come light years in its effectiveness as a fast and simple way to pay our people globally, and our human resources team can accomplish payroll with a few clicks. Today we also use Payoneer, Transferwise, and even Western Union where PayPal cannot serve us.

If you are old enough, like me, to remember walking into the lobby of a prestigious international firm, then you will remember seeing multiple clocks on the wall to allow for time translations across all of the firm's global operations. As I like to say, it's 9 am somewhere. I think, really, they were as much a status symbol for these firms as they were a utilitarian device. For us, it's simple. Every staff member has an international clock on their PCs, laptops, or smartphones which show the time across all of their colleagues' nations. As obvious and basic as that might sound, I cannot express enough what a difference it makes in scheduling real-time conference calls between Manilla, Kiev, New Delhi, New York, and China.

I'll never forget when I was once on a business trip with my teams in India. We were out eating some fantastic food on a Friday night in Delhi. It was about 9 pm. My colleagues started having side conversations about business when it finally dawned on my jet-lagged brain that they had started the U.S. workday just then, while here I was hardly able to keep my eyes open and just wanted to rip more tears of my chili chicken. Oh, it was hot. Hotter than any Indian food you'll get in the U.S.

Summary

Building a global team of professionals can be one of the best things you'll ever do to propel your business forward in today's globally-connected business climate. To be certain, it's an uphill climb; however, accessing the right talent through a disciplined approach, going to great lengths to build human connections, and doing all that is possible to close the geographical and time zone divides will eventually result in what could be a staff member sitting right outside your office. Approach it like you do any other aspect of your business when you initially plan its build. Expect bumps, forks in the road, and steep hills. Once you see the rewards of a global staff, you'll wish you had pursued it much sooner.

CHAPTER 11

NAVIGATING CHANGE IN THE MUSIC INDUSTRY

By **LA'SHION ROBINSON**

Change is inevitable in any industry, but certainly so in the music industry. The key is strategy. I have learned over the years that by focusing on three key ideas, you can define a strategy for your personal musical story and stay relevant in the music industry. I will define for you my ideas and the perspectives of independent artists that I currently work with.

But, before I go any further, I need to level with you: music is a passion that runs through your veins. It is something that moves you…your story becomes the verses of your own personal song. If that does not resonate with you and define your passion, stop reading. Why? Because this chapter will not help you on your journey. I can tell you without a doubt, you will not succeed. It is not easy. Quite honestly, it is hard. I speak from personal experience.

I have failed. Let that sink in. I own it. I have had to close up shop. But I have also grown from those periods of defeat. I studied my failures to understand how to restart and take a smarter, more realistic approach. I researched and applied business models to my passion. I took the approach of combining my entrepreneurial passion with a business model approach to define what success looks like for me.

What I came to realize through reflection on my experiences was that I kept coming back to three common themes.

So, with that spirit and drive as your baseline, let's talk about how **resilience, never be normal, and seizing new opportunities** will keep you relevant in the music industry. I would like to share with you how I penned a new chapter in my musical story and titled it **HUDL Music.** Are you ready? Let's go!

Photo by Rashidah De Vore
L. Robinson (Instagram: @l_hudlmusic)

Resilience

Like so many, I, too, began with aspirations of becoming a successful artist in the music industry. However, once I was in it, I quickly learned that I did not have the talent to become the next Shawn Carter. While in the studio creating and promoting CDs (how many of you actually know what those are?), I discovered a part of the business that I enjoyed more than being an actual artist; I found that I was a better advocate for the artist. As a result, I launched my own record label and had regional success across Alabama, Georgia, and Florida. I thought I had it all figured out. I was convinced I was going to be the next major record label out of the dirty South, bringing in a unique sound. That did not happen. Reality hit.

I had amazing talent on the label, but they had setbacks and I was not at a skill level to help them manage through their stories. I was devastated to lose not only my label but the artists as well. I realized I did not have the maturity to lead and develop a record label. Out of money and resources, I made the decision to shutter my label, putting an end to that chapter. I was not sure what to do next.

With no real business education, I found myself looking for a job where I could learn through hands-on experience. Several years in, I found myself thriving in a fast-paced business environment, working for a Fortune 100 company. Success was born in me. I do not know what it means to be down and out and stay in that moment. I quickly showcased my value and was promoted through the ranks at a rapid pace, leading to senior management level.

However, my passion for the music industry never left me. The flame continued to burn in the background. The average person would have moved on and let their dreams fade, but I remained resilient. I'm a man who is able to withstand and recover from the most difficult situations and come out better for them. During this time of growth is where I mastered the art of business. I learned the structure, planning process, operations mindset, and how to flawlessly execute.

The lessons I learned in corporate America prepared me to make another run at my entrepreneurial passion. This time, I knew I would be prepared with a solid foundation defined in business and management acumen backed with my passion for music. This is how **HUDL Music** came to life. **HUDL Music** is a platform where independent artists have the power to get discovered by an international fanbase. My first interview was with an NYC-based duo. They shared their story of why being resilient is what kept them in the industry for so long. As the music industry changed, they did, too. They had experienced all the setbacks that most independent artists experience from poor management, rejection, and the most common challenge, the lack of financial backing to promote and grow their fanbase. Let's keep it real, most people would have given up, but they persevered and are still in the game, embracing technology and putting out new music on a regular basis. If you want to be successful, you must be resilient and find new ways to make your goals happen. Be resilient.

Photo by Jonathan Guzman (Instagram: @twlv20)
Left: Mike City (Instagram: @done&city), Middle: L. Robinson (Instagram: @l_hudlmusic), Right: Doñe (Instagram: @done&city)

Never Be Normal

What does this mean? It means that to stay relevant in an era of social media that is constantly changing, you must be three steps ahead of your competition. Let your creative thought process run on overdrive. If you can think of it, imagine how to bring it to life. Why should you limit yourself, as an independent artist, to the typical way of making a name for yourself?

Independent artists historically make the majority of their money doing local shows and selling merchandise. In an already oversaturated market of creators, artists must begin to think with the mindset of never being "normal." Normal is boring anyway.

I recently met an artist who knows what it means to never be normal. He created, produced, and mastered his own album. That is way out of the norms for an independent artist. He established a new definition of hustle and put his name on it. He is writing his own story. It is the drive and spirit that I referenced earlier in the chapter that defines him.

The music industry as a whole is in the never normal era, where the unpredictable can and does occur. For example, twelve months ago, no one imagined there would be drive-in concerts or artists from all over the world competing for fans on live streams. At this very moment, the music industry is being defined by abnormal actions to stay relevant to the fans. Not to mention, a social responsibility that many artists feel to their local community, nation, and world. It is becoming part of the brand of an artist.

As I build my interview files, I am often asked how to become successful as an artist. My response in this never normal environment is to develop good business skills because you cannot afford to go out and find a good manager. Side note, a good manager will find you. Next, you have to understand the basics of project management. Understanding the business is not enough. There are way too many artists that undervalue this skillset. Artists that can master operational tasks and some basic project management skills will have a leg up on those that are still stuck with the OG mentality, hustling the way it was done in years past.

Finally, understand the concept of marketing. This has always been important to labels and now it is even more vital for an artist to learn how to market themselves in never normal times. It is not just about posting to social media; it is understanding how to connect with fans in a data-based approach and learning the value of collaboration with other artists and sharing like experiences. It is learning how to tell your story. Fans today want to know what you stand for. They want to understand your social connection. Marketing is in the artists' hands and with the help of **HUDL Music** running promotion and distribution through music streaming platforms, which lowers the barrier to entry, you have the opportunity to be exposed to the world. That is never normal.

Photo by Jonathan Guzman (Instagram: @twlv20)
Left: L. Robinson (Instagram: @l_hudlmusic),
Right: Nuutrino (Instagram: @nuutrino)

Seizing New Opportunities

The definition of seizing new opportunities is "to act quickly in order to use an opportunity that may not be available later." Now more than ever, during the health crisis of 2020, the music industry has learned how dependent they are on sold out, live concerts. With thousands of fans screaming and vibing to the music, a connection is instantly made to the artist and we are reminded why there is a connection. Now, with that option taken off the table, the opportunity to seize a new idea is ready for the taking.

Mindset is key. The idea that independent artists cannot do local performances or attend open mics is a closed-minded thought process. It is a new opportunity for the taking. The opportunity was created as a circumstance to an unforeseen challenge. Visualize a platform of music sharing, of direct communication to the artists, just a click away from their merchandise site…that is the idea that came to fruition by **HUDL Music** in this current crisis.

Independent artists now have an opportunity to share their talent directly with music lovers who are looking for something new, creative, and a break from the mold. The key to success in the music industry is the willingness to take a risk. To think outside of the box and make your dream a reality.

I recently spoke to an independent artist who had a successful career in the early 2000s with an R&B group. Due to actions out of his control, he found himself starting a solo career, with the knowledge that he did not want a mainstream label. Record labels are not what they once were; artists now want the ability to seize opportunities like never before. The slow march to extinction continues for traditional record labels, giving rise to a more independent approach to making it in the music industry.

As mentioned earlier, **HUDL Music** was created because there was an opportunity to help independent artists launch their careers alongside other independent artists without competing with the demands of major record labels. As the R&B artist and I continued our discussion, we talked about the opportunities that exist for independent artists in this new time. What was most important to him was retaining creative control over his music, more control over his career, and being able to make pivots faster, as well as being ahead of the curve by using technology. This is the challenge I believe artists in the music industry should try to solve: How will you create the opportunity to stand out? Remember, the aspects of the entertainment industry no longer exist as we knew them to be. Take this time to seize a new opportunity which supports your dream. Now is the time.

Photo by Jonathan Guzman (Instagram: @twlv20)
Left: L. Robinson (Instagram: @l_hudlmusic),
Right: Lenny Harold (Instagram: @lennyharold)

The music industry is not for the faint of heart. As I said, it is hard. It is not easy. But it is absolutely worth it if you have resilience, the never normal mindset, and the thought process to normalize seizing new opportunities. Approach your musical passion like a business, not a hobby. Determine your goals, define them, and build a strategy. Let your passion for music keep the flame burning and do not stay down if you run into hard times. Pivot. Take advantage of the lesson placed in front of you and learn a new skill to carry you into the next musical chapter of your story. Then, make more music.

I do have one ask of you: allow **HUDL Music** to join you as you write the next verse. Give your independent music career the opportunity it deserves to grow while you maintain control, all while getting exposure to a fanbase you have earned. I told you my story, now go create yours. **HUDL Music** is here to help guide you through the plot of becoming the next fierce, independent artist.

Photo by Jonathan Guzman (Instagram: @twlv20)
Left: Curt Cuscino (Instagram: @thatcuscinosound),
Right: L. Robinson (Instagram: @l_hudlmusic)

CHAPTER 12

EVERY COMPANY SHOULD HAVE A DIVERSE BOARD

By **MARTIN ROWINSKI**

Every company needs to have a diversified board of advisors or board of directors. Every single one. It does not matter if yours is a public or private organization, a board is a necessary step in growing and scaling a business.

Before starting my own company, Boardsi, in 2018, I worked for and consulted for many corporations over the course of my career. I've worked with huge organizations with both types of boards and smaller companies with upper management acting as advisors to the President or CEO.

When you think of a board of directors, what is the first thing that comes to mind? Maybe a big group of rich, old white men who are all former CEOs of large companies?

But it is imperative to have a diverse board made up of people of different genders, races, ages, experiences, and careers.

Here's why: A board is meant to advise or direct the company's leaders. If they all come from the same industry or career trajectory or educational background, they'll all advise you in the same general way. They'll think the same and want the company to maintain the status quo.

With a board of similar people, you are missing out on the creativity and differing perspectives that can truly push your company in new directions and to new heights.

Let's backtrack for a moment.

The Differences

A Board of Directors (BOD) is common and you are likely familiar with the concept. This board has legally defined responsibilities, are often elected by the shareholders, and are in place to make decisions and help lead and direct the company's CEO and leadership team. The BOD is not running the company; instead, they are a system of checks and balances for the organization's leadership, similar to the way the government is run.

The board members have a duty to the organization as a whole, not to individual employees, meaning they have a responsibility to put the big-picture organizational needs and shareholder's needs over those of the employees. The BOD members can be sued personally for any mistakes, and are more legal-specific, meaning they are involved in human resources and compliance.

A Board of Advisors (BOA) is typically an external team of people and is more informal. They do not have specific legal or compliance responsibilities and are picked by the company's leadership team to advise, counsel, and mentor them. They are not liable to any shareholders, and cannot be held personally liable for mistakes, so BOAs are not required to have expensive directors and officers liability

(D&O) insurance. Their main goal is only to help the management team with fresh perspectives and ideas to grow.

As you can see, there are distinct differences between the two types of boards. At first glance, it may seem more beneficial to have a BOA only, as they are easier to create, less costly, not personally liable, and only there to help the management team. However, both board types can be extremely beneficial to any size organization.

One practical example is the current COVID19 pandemic. BODs have played a critical role in helping companies navigate through it. One responsibility of a Board of Directors is to have emergency plans created for the company - even unprecedented ones. They must be flexible and adaptable and bring perspective to the company's leadership. Many larger, well-known companies were surprised by the pandemic and did not have a clear direction or know how to respond initially. Because of this lack of preparation, it took some companies longer to figure out what to do and implement it. Other companies were prepared for different potential situations and already had the emergency plans written and created and only needed to implement them, so they were able to respond much more quickly.

Think about it: If your company does not typically have employees work from home, what tools, software, and hardware would be required for the entire workforce to be able to work from home in the case of a pandemic or other emergency? How quickly could you get the things you require, issue hardware, train employees on how to use the systems, and get everyone back to 100% productivity?

That clearly shows how important emergency preparedness plans are - and those are often the responsibility of the BOD.

Size and Structure of Boards

In most cases, BODs have around 10 members. Too many people on the board may make it harder for them to come to a consensus, which is necessary when leading the leaders. Board members often have a specific area of expertise, such as cybersecurity, legal, etc.

BOAs, on the other hand, do not need to come to a consensus and can be as small or large as you want. Ten is still a nice number and is often used. You can also have multiple advisors for different areas of expertise. These boards are generally more creative and ideas-based that BODs.

When it comes to the structure of boards and the individual time and monetary commitment, every deal is different. There are some general numbers to know, though. A member of a BOD is often expected to put in 200 or more hours per year serving the board and the company. An advisor, however, is making less of a time commitment, generally around 40-50 hours per year.

When it comes to paying board members, there are three common types of deals:

- A simple financial deal where you pay the board member hourly for the time they put in.
- Equity deals, where board members are compensated with a percentage of the company (especially effective if the company is planning an IPO or exit strategy).
- A combination of both.

There are also cases where an organization is looking for funding and they will pursue a board member who has or can get capital for the company. This is completely legal and is similar to bringing on a partner. This person would likely sit on the BOD and get a larger percentage of equity than other board members.

Diversity Rules

Diversified boards are crucial. You do not want to be the type of leader who can't think outside the box or implement creative solutions. And you also want to make sure you're in compliance and following all regulations and running a company that benefits its shareholders.

If everyone on the board is Ivy-league-educated, around the same age, is the same race and gender, and has about the same experience, you will have a group of people who think similarly. A great board is one where the members challenge each other, think differently, come from different perspectives, and each brings something unique to the table.

Age does not matter. A young tech startup founder will bring different skills and ideas to the table than an older retired judge or a person with 30 years of experience in your same industry. You want all of those people! One person may push for change and growth and another may be more guarded and protective of the company, so a mix of the two can help you get the best results and create a strategic growth plan for your organization.

Instead of focusing on their age or education level, look at their successes. Look for successful people regardless of age, race, gender, or industry. Bring together interesting, creative people who are passionate about what you're doing. Allow for as many perspectives and experience levels as possible - that is what will give you the diversity you need.

Focus on their personality traits and try to have a balance. For example, try to have a mix of the four main personality types: analysts, diplomats, sentinels, and explorers. Also, look for "soft" skills like having high emotional intelligence and mindful intelligence in addition to being traditionally "smart." Soft skills infuse a level of maturity to the board, which trickles down to the leadership team. Having a balance leads to a more holistic and well-rounded board - which is best for your company.

Some leadership teams don't want a diverse board because it could generate competing viewpoints, friction, and conflict. But with varying viewpoints comes valuable insights and new ideas, built on a foundation of success. Any smart leader or CEO knows their company will benefit from multiple points of view and that they will themselves learn and become an even better leader.

How to Build a Diverse Board

You're ready to create a diverse leadership team to help devise superior strategies and bring new mindsets and viewpoints to your company. How do you do it?

When it comes to the board of directors, start with having a specific purpose when picking a board member. Maybe you need insights and expertise on cybersecurity. Direct your search toward cybersecurity experts who have consulting experience. This way, you are not just getting theoretical knowledge, you're getting practical knowledge and guidance on the actual implementation.

If you want to go public or need to plan an exit strategy, look for board members who have successfully gone public with a company or guided companies through exits. If you don't have anyone with this specific experience, then you have a hole in your board and will miss out on the needed guidance and help in that area.

For the board of advisors, look for people worth consulting. Be wary of only looking for a widely respected household name. While their name may be beneficial to your company, they still need to have useful input and relevant experience to help you meet your goals. You're not looking for a spokesperson or an ambassador, you're looking for great advice.

For both boards, recruit only the people you want to listen to and are actually planning to take their advice. Having a specific "type" of person in mind is fine, but use your instincts and get people you want to work with and will listen to.

Going into your search with specific ideas of the expertise you may be missing or need more of will not only create a stronger board for your company but will also keep you from making expensive missteps and spending your own time researching those areas or money hiring additional people internally to fill a hole.

Specifically go into your search with the mindset of finding different types of people from various industries, with varying levels of experience. Do not limit your search for diversity to only race and sex. Look for skills, successes, and their drive. And don't worry about age, either. Age is just a number! A bright, young, successful entrepreneur is going to bring different ideas to the table than a man with 35 years of experience in your same industry. It is becoming more and more common to have younger people on BOAs - even BODs are starting to trend younger!

Think of the interesting ideas you'll get from your board when you have both a young tech startup founder AND the banking CFO. They'll both be able to brainstorm and work to find creative solutions, plus you'll get the benefits of their success and experiences.

Recruiting Board Members

Recruiting board members is similar to recruiting a new employee. When searching, make sure to clearly communicate with candidates and only talk to those who understand the time commitment you're asking for. Not everyone has the time or wants to put in the work to be an advisor; you don't want a member who is overcommitted and not able to put in the time. I recently had someone come to me asking me to be on their BOA, but they wanted me to commit 200 hours per year - that simply is not an option for me right now!

In the recruiting process, you'll also need to be careful of any conflicts of interest.

Like hiring a new employee in your organization, you have two options for recruiting: Do it yourself or hire a specialized agency.

My company, Boardsi, is a highly specialized recruiting agency specific to board members. We have a wide network of executives and professionals who are interested in board membership and already understand the commitment a board requires. We handle all the vetting and pre-interview for you and present you with great candidates that actually meet your needs. We aim to save you the hassle and time of conducting the search on your own. Your time is better used interviewing the people you know can make the difference and not searching for candidates who may not even have the time or interest. Within weeks, you can be talking to the right people versus months searching on your own.

I created Boardsi after leaving a position in a company where the CEO would sit with his advisors and talk at them. For 90% of every meeting, he was the one talking. Whenever an advisor had an idea, the CEO would either ignore it or claim the credit. I left and began consulting again while looking for a potential board opportunity.

I networked a lot and met with companies but I felt like I just wasn't finding the *right* opportunity. When researching a recruiting firm to help me, I found a couple based in the UK but weirdly, none in the U.S. So, in 2018, we started one. In addition to our highly qualified talent, we use artificial intelligence and other technology to match personnel with great companies.

All of my experience and networking has helped me build out a network of people who guide me - my own advisors. One of them has such significant experience with boards that he published a book on the subject and helped us create training materials for the business.

Boardsi was not just created to fill a hole in the market but is also designed to help businesses and leadership teams reach their goals. Having a diverse and interesting board is an important part of building a successful business and accomplishing your goals faster and with preparedness and creativity.

Do you need a board member? Or are you looking to become a member of a board? We can help! Reach out at info@boardsi.com.

CHAPTER 13

CROSSING THE LINE

By **MICHAEL RALBY**

My name is Michael Ralby, and probably much like you, I have worn many hats in my life. I have been a son, brother, husband, father, ex-husband, significant other, friend, mentor, entrepreneur, athlete, yoga enthusiast, chef, and a trusted financial advisor in the securities industry. Like you, I have inherent strengths, weakness, interests, and disinterests which have defined my life path. Our choices are impacted by external events and the influence of others. It doesn't matter if we have encountered these people by fate, chance, design, or misfortune; what is relevant is how we deal with the impact their actions have on our lives.

In my youth, if someone would have told me I would become a wildly successful bond broker, I would have been flabbergasted. Had someone told me that I would work for and with some of the most notorious players in that industry, I would have not believed them. If someone told me that I would able to cultivate highly rewarding client relationships - and navigate their investments through the market crashes of 1987, 1993 and 1994, 9/11, the 2008 housing crisis, and the rash of high-profile Ponzi schemes of the late 2000s - with little or no damage to their portfolios, I would have been rendered speechless.

And if someone would have told me that in 2016, a petty incident based on a fairly inconsequential 2009 situation would lead me to abandon my 30+ year career, I would have been incredulous.

I have learned that the unimaginable is, in fact, imaginable, and all of the above did happen.

In 2017, my situation felt surreal, empty, and unfair. In April of 2020, as I write this chapter, the global community is in the grips of a pandemic. With time to reflect, I can acknowledge the fact that my professional life was molded and then twisted, by a series of highly unlikely encounters and events outside of my control.

As with any good story, the best place to start is at the beginning. My parents, Howard and Marilyn, were originally from Boston, Massachusetts. My dad served in the United States Navy during World War II. In 1954, he met my mother and they were married in 1955. In 1956, they decided to relocate to Miami, Florida where they soon began their family. My sister, Elyse, and I both adored our parents.

My dad was the sun around which my world rotated. He was an extraordinary person. Even-tempered, quick with a joke, honest, and curious. For many years, he owned Miami Auto Radiators and our family prospered. He always wanted the best for his family, and in his forties, he made a bold career change and entered the securities industry. He moved up quickly and became the managing broker of a local EF Hutton branch. I was proud of my dad and his accomplishments. However, while I aspired to possess his personal and moral traits, I was not inspired to follow in his professional footsteps.

When I was young, people were unfamiliar with neurodiversity. They did not understand what individuals who had "different brains" needed to assimilate and thrive. As a population, they were largely misunderstood and often felt like square pegs in round holes. My challenge was being born a "lefty" in a world of "righties." I was forced to learn to do things with my right hand, which felt inorganic, uncomfortable, and unnatural. To me, the world often seemed confusing, illogical, and most importantly, backward. My parents pushed me to attend college, but I was disengaged and frustrated with academia. I survived four years of university by focusing on my interest in sports, after which I spent time on the professional tennis circuit.

In 1984, not long after concluding my less-than-stellar athletic career, I was playing tennis at the country club. A man approached me and asked if I was Howard Ralby's son. I came to learn that he was a founding partner of a small and highly successful bond firm. He proceeded to tell me how much he liked and respected my father. He invited me to visit First Miami Securities and I accepted. This random encounter changed my life. During the tour of the office, I was struck by the staff's energy level, the overall excitement, and numerous status symbols displayed with pride.

More importantly, on that visit, I crossed an intellectual line. Their world of symbols and numbers made sense to me. The inherent competitiveness of their industry resonated with me. I was able to see patterns, anomalies, and opportunities all around me. From that moment on, I was hooked on the brokerage business. The first year was a learning curve, but by year four I was among their top producers. I carved a niche for myself by specializing in high-quality bonds. I loved the personal interaction with the clients and the cache of being a "trusted advisor."

The Brokerage Business

Some readers may not be familiar with finance or the brokerage business. Others may have knowledge derived from the news or Hollywood movies. These stories tend to center around the competitive, exciting, lucrative world of saints and sinners who made or lost their careers on "the street." There are a few things to keep in mind to understand the brokerage industry and my story:

- The one thing that remains constant is the fact that all brokerage firms' primary objective is to generate money from the investor.
- Over the years, the rules of the securities industry game have changed many times. Two entities enforce the rules. One is the Financial Industry Regulatory Authority (FINRA), a non-governmental organization that regulates member brokerage firms and exchange markets. They handle regulation, enforcement, and arbitration operations of the New York Stock Exchange. The second entity is the Securities and Exchange Commission (SEC), which is an independent agency of the federal government. The SEC holds primary responsibility for enforcing the federal securities laws, proposing securities rules, and regulating the securities industry.
- The bond market and the stock market have an inverse relationship. When stocks are up, bonds are down and vice versa. There are only two ways to lose money in the bond market: interest rate risks and credit risks. High-quality bonds are traditionally low-risk investments.
- The industry has its own terminology. The "line" generally refers to gross profit. "Above the line" refers to sales less the cost of goods. "Below the line" are operating expenses, interest, and taxes. A "book of business" refers to an advisor's

client list. "Upfront money" is bonus money paid to relocate professionals for their book of business upon signing. "Back end money" is incentive dollars paid to relocating advisors at the end of a specific time period as accounts move from one firm to another. A "clearinghouse" is an intermediary between buyers and sellers of financial instruments.

I remained at First Miami Securities (FMS) as a Senior Vice President until 1990. Overall, it was a very happy and profitable time. The 1987 market crash and all subsequent market crashes and scandals had the following impacts on the business:

1. Advisors spent a huge amount of time reassuring and calming clients.
2. There was a major shift from branch managers mentoring and protecting their advisors to protecting the firm's bottom line.
3. Compliance became much more stringent, complex, and adversarial toward the advisors.
4. The compensation model shifted from being commission-based to fee-based, and Wall Street advisors took a huge pay cut. The new mantra was to gather assets.
5. Advisors became extremely wary of management and distrust was prevalent.

It was then that I began to question certain information I heard, to have doubts about the trustworthiness of leadership, and to feel that the line was blurring. I was not alone. At the end of my tenure, seven of the nine FMS advisors moved on. I took my book of business to the bond industry powerhouse, Smith Barney, while all six others joined Prudential Securities.

1990 – 2002 was a remarkable period both professionally and personally. I remained at Smith Barney building my business until 1995. I had the privilege to build a relationship with one of the industry's biggest producers and we became lifelong friends. He would always tell me, "You will never get wealthy in life working for someone else," and encouraged me to start my own firm. So, that is what I did. I founded Ralby Asset Management just as my ex-wife, Elise, and I began welcoming our sons, Max and Noah, into the world one at a time.

We were living in Aventura, Florida and the area was experiencing high growth. Elise and I felt our children would benefit from moving to a smaller community. We relocated to Boca Raton, and simultaneously JW Genesis Securities approached me about a potential merger. I knew the founder well and believed they were building something of value. I was well aware that I could contribute to their model but not create it on my own. With that realization, the two organizations become one. Later, this firm was acquired twice more and ended up as part of Wells Fargo Securities.

With the first acquisition, I once again began to feel uneasy with the new management and continued to see changes in the industry that I intrinsically knew were harbingers of darker days to come. In 2002, I departed JW Genesis, taking my original RAL team with me, and started Above the Line Consulting. We gained traction quickly but could not raise the necessary capital required to sustain ourselves. Not long after, I got a call from the Houston, Texas-based Stanford Financial Group (SFG). Their founders wished to start an office in Boca Raton and they wished for Above the Line Consulting to join them. This was incredibly exciting, as SFG was the talk of the street in 2005. They had an incredible system, were recruiting top-producing brokers from across the country, had a sterling reputation, and they vetted out. By 2009, I was managing a multi-million-dollar book of business and the future looked bright.

However, all was not as it seemed. We found out the hard way in February of 2009, when the SEC raided all Stanford Financial Group offices, including ours, and closed them.

The Beginning of the End

According to press reports and court documents, Allen Stanford crossed the line at least a decade prior. He was convicted of running a Ponzi scheme involving 18,000 investors. The Stanford scam, second only to Madoff's in size, involved billions in fraudulent certificates of deposits. Sadly, unlike Madoff's victims, most of the Stanford targets were never compensated.

On a micro level, the SEC froze all of Stanford's investor assets. On a macro level, the banking and financial crisis was aggravated by Stanford, Madoff, and a few other fraudsters of note, and FINRA could not manage the situation. Their response was to enact costly and complex compliance mandates. The brokerage firm's response was to change their compensation plans from commission-based to fee-based models. They went from a model that dictated an arbitrary estimated portion of the commission revenue needed to be earmarked for litigation and compliance costs to a fee-based model that guaranteed a predictable set income figure to offset those costs. Long story short, brokers took a massive pay cut so the brokerage firms could try to survive the tsunami of lawsuits and compliance costs in the first decade of the 2000s.

In hindsight, and despite the fact that I was in no way involved in the Ponzi scheme, I should have seen the writing on the wall and sought out another career right then. I did not. With the freezing of the assets and the closing of the office, my fellow advisors and I began to seek out other career opportunities. Oppenheim & Co. made a deal with the SEC to bring us over. However, they were smart, and instead of the traditional upfront money for bringing our books of business, they offered us back-end money payable at the end of each calendar year for a determined contract period. When the SEC froze the Stanford investor assets, our managed portfolio revenue decreased by approximately 70%. By the time my contract was nearly completed, I am proud to say the majority of my clients remained with me and the original value of their combined portfolios was intact.

When I was at Stanford, I secured a client who later became someone I thought was a friend. He followed me to Oppenheimer and later to Morgan Stanley. Jack was an unusual fellow with a unique personality. He tied his sense of self-worth to starting arguments - valid or not - with others. He particularly liked to involve authority figures in his disputes. Threatening his targets with litigation or the filing of formal complaints with professional licensing agencies was a large part of his methodology. Jack would create drama wherever he could. He was also fond of alcohol. It was routine for him to call me while drunk and rail against this or that at length any time of day, seven days a week. His skirmishes were always tied to a perceived lack of respect or the principal of the thing rather than the issue itself. Abusive cruelty was in his DNA, and no one was immune from his wrath if he felt he had been wronged or insulted.

The biggest mistake I have made in my life was thinking Jack would not attack me because I was his friend and advisor. Attack me he did, and that battle changed the trajectory of my life.

Income became a challenge for me. I was in the midst of a divorce, my children needed tuition, I had bills to pay, and my back-end bonus was months away. Security regulations state that an advisor can't borrow money from a client, but it is within the lines to get a third-party loan with a client co-signer as long as the broker gets permission from their manager and a letter was placed in their file. I was reluctant to go to firm management as I was distrustful and frustrated with the system, so I looked for a loophole and I reached out to my "friend" Jack for help. I arranged for him to meet with me at my bank to obtain a loan predicated on him being a co-signer. I got the loan and in one year and a day, the note was paid in full plus interest. A year later, I ran short again and we went through the same loan process. This time the amount and the time frame were reduced. This loan was paid back 31 days later in full with interest. Where I pushed the line and violated the rule, was that I didn't disclose the loan. I did not disclose it because of my previously-noted distrust. It turned out my instincts were correct because later my manager from Oppenheimer was barred; he and his superior were both suspended from the industry for one year for fraud.

In 2013, we had seen the bond market rebound, we had rebuilt our business at Oppenheimer, and we began to look for other opportunities when one presented itself at Morgan Stanley. I was very happy there, as Bob was an excellent manager and a great leader. Sadly, Bob moved on with the branch's top producer to another firm. Eventually, Dave, a regional manager, stepped down to become the manager of the Boca Raton office. Dave was not a proper fit for this branch, and as a result, 30 brokers left the firm, and Dave was demoted and moved to a significantly smaller market.

An important initiative for Morgan Stanley was building its banking business. They created a program where if a client direct-deposited funds a set number of times per year using a specified charge card, the firm would reimburse their annual credit card usage fee. Jack was enrolled in that program. Shortly before Bob left, Jack missed the direct deposit and his fee was not rebated. He called every day screaming and carrying on over a few hundred dollars. Bob agreed to rebate Jack's fee, and I reassured him I would get it corrected. But when Bob left, the promise went unfulfilled by Dave. As you can imagine, Jack went out of his mind, and this is when my friend of seven years turned on me with a ferocity the likes of which one cannot imagine. He told Dave about the past loans he'd co-signed, and Morgan Stanley began a one-year internal investigation; I was exonerated. This infuriated Jack, who then went to FINRA and filed a complaint.

Defending a FINRA complaint is a complex, time-consuming, stressful, and expensive process. I felt cornered and my only options were to fight, quit, or be fired. I dealt with the system for about a year with no support from management. The line had closed behind me, and in 2018, I decided to quit. My only regret about my decision is that it cost me my relationships with the wonderful people I had advised for over 30 years and considered to be friends.

Moving Forward & Reinventing

Over the last two years, I have created a new world for myself in business development. Businesses I've worked with include Tal Kimmel at mIR Scientific, a ground-breaking prostate screening test using urine rather than blood and it's 99% accurate; an organization in the telemedicine space and my partnership with Arminda Figueroa; my work with Steve Nudelberg on a joint venture company called On the Money; and YipTV, working with co-founders Michael Tribolet and Chuck Gaspari. YipTV is a patented live-streaming service aimed at consumers of Spanish and English content in Latin America for a minimal monthly subscription fee. All of these endeavors bring me great joy both personally and professionally. Now, when the phone rings with issues and challenges, they are related to what I have manifested and not what I have inherited from outside influencers.

What has transpired has been the greatest blessing of my life aside from my sons, Max and Noah. These two remarkable young men have excelled in every endeavor they have undertaken. I could not be prouder of the contributions they have made to our society. I am also deeply appreciative of Marissa - my life partner - whose strength, love, and loyalty has comforted and encouraged me through thick and thin. These three mean everything to me. I also wish to thank all of the people who have remained in my circle of influence, and I do wish to especially acknowledge my dear friends and family for all of their love and support.

CHAPTER 14

WHAT IS A PERSONAL CFO?

By **ROBERT WOLF**

In this chapter, I want to talk to you about why every business owner or high-income earner needs a personal CFO. But before I explain what a personal CFO is and what we do, I believe it is important to understand some of the mindset of why this is important to you.

The first key is to run your personal life like a business and stop running your business like your personal life. This comes at the suggestion of the IRS. Now, they don't come right out and say this but if you think about the old adage "follow the money," this becomes apparent.

You see, the IRS is in the business of taxing income. That is all they do, tax income. The question then is what creates income and the simple answer is assets. Assets create income. The what, when, why, where, and how you get that income depends on the type of asset you want and how the IRS treats each of the three stages of that asset.

So, if an asset creates income then we can make the argument that you are an asset. In fact, you are the only asset of all of them which has a brain. So, that means we need to run you as the key asset, so we need to run you as You, Inc.

All other assets, including your business, is an asset of You, Inc. You are in charge of giving every other asset a purpose and a job of why they belong in the You, Inc. business. Let me explain further. Why does everyone save money for retirement in retirement accounts?

The answer is in the name of the account, "retirement account." You see, that money, also an asset, was given a purpose, so we save in retirement accounts to keep it earmarked for its purpose. The same should be true of all other assets.

I could literally go on and on and turn this chapter into a book, so I will switch gears to why You, Inc. needs a personal CFO.

There are two mindsets a business owner should have:
1. The mindset of the owner of the business
2. The mindset of an employee of the business

These shifts in mindset are exactly how the IRS views you as a business owner.

The IRS is an investment partner with business owners. They give owners tax deductions, tax incentives, tax credits, and tax rebates. There are four areas of tax benefits sprinkled all over the tax code to allow you as a business owner to reduce your tax savings.

Why would the IRS do this? Well think about it, if you increase your cash flow due to a reduction in taxes what are you going to do with that extra cash flow? That's right, put it right back into the business. The IRS knows that because they know you and I, as business owners, are addicted to our businesses.

When we put enough of the cash flow into our business and our business grows, then what happens when you as the owner can't do all the tasks necessary to run your business? That's right, hire employees.

That is the income revenue the IRS is looking for! You see, as a W2 employee, your tax reduction strategies are comprised of the Schedule A (itemized deductions) in the 1040 personal tax return.

Don't get me wrong, if you as a business owner are overpaying on income taxes, the IRS isn't going to refund you money if you don't know how to understand their language.

What are you left with then? Trying to either figure out the tax code on your own, hiring a CPA (which you already have), or whatever creative idea you may come up with.

Here is the interesting thing about the IRS. Remember how I said they are your best business partner? Think about this: if you have a business partner would you want that partner to be reckless and immature about your business dealings? Of course not!

Why is the IRS any different? They aren't. So, they want you to protect their investment and they will give you opportunities to reduce your taxes. Why would they do this?

Again, if they can bank on the predictable revenue stream (W2 employee income tax revenue), then they can report back to Congress their revenue and Congress can "budget" (I used quotes because there is no budget in the word budget when it comes to Congress).

The big question is how do we do this? Great question. This leads us to what we do as your personal CFO. To answer that, I am going to answer each of the following questions:

- What is a Chief Financial Officer (CFO)?
- What does a CFO do?
- What are the benefits of being a CFO?
- What do we do as your personal CFO?
- Who should have a personal CFO?
- What are the benefits and advantages of having a personal CFO?
- How does a personal CFO get paid?
- What's the difference between a financial advisor, CPA, and investment manager?

What Is a Chief Financial Officer?

A chief financial officer (CFO) is the senior executive responsible for managing the financial actions of a company. The CFO's duties include tracking cash flow and financial planning, as well as analyzing the company's financial strengths and weaknesses and proposing corrective actions.

The CFO is responsible for managing finances and accounting and ensuring that the company's financial reports are accurate.

What Does a CFO do?

The CFO reports to the chief executive officer (CEO) but has significant input in the company's investments, capital structure, and how the company manages its income and expenses. The CFO works with other senior managers and plays a key role in a company's overall success, especially in the long run.

The CFO may assist the CEO with forecasting, cost-benefit analysis, and obtaining funding for various initiatives. In the financial industry, a CFO is the highest-ranking position, and in other industries, it is usually the third-highest position in a company.

What Are The Benefits of Being a CFO?

The CFO role is a strategic partner to the CEO. The CFO plays a vital role in influencing company strategy, including managing how the planning of cash flow coincides with the business goals and growth projections.

Having a personal CFO means you have someone to work with any of the other professional advisors you have so that you as a business owner can focus on the business and its strengths.

What Do We Do as Your Personal CFO?

The answer to this question is based on the individuality of the owner and the business and what the desired accomplishments are. But before we can strive for those accomplishments, we first need to understand the current situation. How can changes or adjustments be made without understanding what is being done currently?

Here are a few tools we use to understand a company's current situation:

- Asset Inventory
- Cash Flow Analysis
- Debt Analysis
- Tax Plan
- Asset Building Plan

Once we have done this analysis then we can formulate how to buddy up each of the assets to another asset to allow for maximum efficiency in growing the assets of You, Inc.

Who Should Have A Personal CFO?

Every business owner or high-income employee needs to have a personal CFO. If you believe in the idea explained at the beginning of this chapter of the mindset of the IRS, then you believe in the idea of embracing the partnership and moving forward with a solution-oriented plan. When working with a solution- and partnership-oriented approach, results are seen immediately.

What Are the Benefits and Advantages of Having a Personal CFO?

I believe this has been thoroughly explained by this point. Having a personal CFO who can help guide You, Inc. in the direction of having not just your business but all of your assets working in unison to a common goal is what generates immediate results.

Understanding how a personal CFO can help give purpose to all those assets within You, Inc. allows us to buddy up the various assets to be most efficient.

How Does a Personal CFO Get Paid?

This question is going to be answered only for our business and not how others work. We get compensated and rewarded based on our success, not on what we say or promise we can do.

The first area is based on a monthly retainer agreement, which some call a subscription model. This investment allows the client to have the comfort of knowing they can call at any time for any question without feeling like they are "bugging" us.

The second area can be based on a percentage of success, meaning instead of a monthly retainer agreement, there can be a revenue share structure. This model is great for those businesses that may have fluctuating periods of the year where a percentage goes to the personal CFO during positive revenue periods and during the periods of the year where there is less revenue, the personal CFO defers revenue share to periods of higher revenue.

Is a Personal CFO the same as a CPA?

The biggest difference is that a personal CFO is in a position to work in conjunction with the business owner to have an unbiased relationship while guiding the owner to their agreed-upon goals.

Keep in mind, though, this is different with each client, so there is not a cookie-cutter plan that works for every business, which is another reason having a personal CFO is beneficial. A customized plan based on the client's situation is key, so when reviewing an investment port-folio or an insurance plan, the personal CFO can help the client focus on the overall goals and how investments and insurance work with that plan.

Many CPAs have limited knowledge in the tax code from a tax planning perspective but have a great knowledge base when it comes to the best way to prepare a tax return and how to maximize the client's tax forms to benefit their business.

Let me explain. You see, most CPAs and other tax professionals I have come across through client interactions or networking are "tax preparers." This means they prepare tax returns for you so you can let your business partner, the IRS, know how your financial health looks during the year of the filed tax return.

You provide all of your documentation to your tax preparer and they enter the information into the software. At times, they can see that you may have an opportunity to take advantage of a deduction here or there, but typically they focus on what we call Non-Appreciable Deductions.

Those are deductions that still provide tax savings but you have to spend money on something that does not grow in value, therefore, a year from now it is not worth more than when you spent money on it. For example, has your tax preparer told you that if you bought a new truck you could get an "x" amount in tax savings? So, what they are saying is if you spend $50,000 you can save $20,000 in taxes. Don't get me wrong, this is still a very important aspect of your overall tax plan but how many trucks do you need?

But if you had the opportunity to reduce your taxes by spending money on something that can grow in value versus not which would you choose? Of course, the deduction that grows in value. We call that an Appreciable Deduction.

The expertise in understanding the various strategies available to use Appreciable Deductions is what we could call a "tax planner."

Which would you prefer?

Of course, you would want the tax planner, but in reality, you need both. You see, the wealthy have tax teams and most small business owners have only one tax person, who happens to be a tax preparer. By adding a personal CFO to your team, you are developing a tax team with expertise in more areas to help reduce your taxes, which is also improving your business's cash flow.

Based on this new understanding of what a personal CFO is and does, what do you think your next steps should be?

CHAPTER 15

HOW TO SUSTAIN MARKET LEADERSHIP WITH TECHNOLOGY

By **SARAH MILLER**

What is the new normal these days? This seems to be a commonly asked question during these unprecedented times. Sustainability and adaptability are key to getting through the lean times and returning to the marketplace so that businesses can retain leadership and brand loyalty. It is now more important than ever to evaluate the core principles of your business and push forward into a marketplace that is hard to navigate while being told to socially distance, which is resulting in industry events moving from in-person to virtual.

While millions of people have been told to hunker down to weather this global storm of uncertainty, business leaders can't overlook the health of their companies, and the ever-present need to rely more on virtual technology to stay in touch and grow. We all crave human interaction, and we are now forced to find that human connection via other means - all while retaining market leadership and ensuring our businesses are successful and sustainable. So here we are, on our smartphones, tablets, and computers hopefully interacting and communicating in a meaningful and fulfilling way. This is not a bad thing! It provides us more flexibility and more opportunities to connect with teams, clients, partners, and potential customers. Since we are now living in a virtual world, we need to take advantage of existing and emerging technology that helps us to stay connected within the global community.

For companies to achieve sustainability in the marketplace, it is critical to be in front of the new technology-driven generation and maintain industry leadership.

Companies today require authority leadership, clear advocacy agendas, and market knowledge to establish global footprints for products and services. We watch market leaders who continuously map the landscape, interpret prevailing conditions, and define new forces and directions. These are the respected voices, credible commentators, trusted advisors, and "go-to" media sources. All of these leaders we watch, listen to, and follow are leaning on technology to stay ahead of the curve. As a CEO, we attract attention by taking PR and market communications to a higher strategic level, challenging traditional thinking, and advocating an arresting point-of-view. As consumers embrace new technologies, companies must become more penetrating, incisive, and articulate about their products, their industry services, and the challenges and requirements in order to grow. The only way to establish footprints and gain market share is by being smart, substantive, informed, and connected.

In the end, we all want to be visionaries, knowledge brokers, and newsmakers, but the big question is how do we do this? We do it by utilizing cutting-edge technologies and leaning on the disruptive technologies there to help set the path to success.

We often ask ourselves how industry leaders become trusted brands that magnetize investors, customers, and the public? Successful leaders engage in these five strategies to keep their companies sustainable in hard times:

1. **Better Brand Loyalty** - Customers are loyal, so it is important to gain their trust early and establish a relationship that the customers can rely upon through good times and bad. A loyal customer may not purchase in volume in lean times, but they will still default to your brand when they need products or services.

2. **Engaging in Experiential Marketing** - Give customers an experience they can touch, see, and/ or relate to. This helps strengthen their brand loyalty to you by promoting similar and empathetic experiences through the products and services offered.

3. **Letting Public Relations Drive** - Public relations is the most effective way to market and create demand for technology brands in a tight economic climate, followed by customer relationship management and brand advertising.

4. **Having a Go-to-Market Strategy** – It is imperative that there is a strategic plan to penetrate the market and drive brand recognition in prosperous times. It is even more critical in economic downturns. Market strategy can vary from integrated marketing campaigns to top strategic PR, but it is crucial to know who you are targeting and what outcome you desire.

5. **Substantive & Flexible Blueprint** – Success relies on execution. However, even the best strategic and creative planning will sometimes run into speed bumps that the markets or consumers throw out. Verify the data and facts that support the technologies the company has chosen and then let tech

help drive the right message out into the marketplace. This will ensure that your company has a better chance of sustaining long-term success.

Embracing technology is critical to help clear the way to thrive and survive in lean times, but combined with creative and strategic PR and go-to-market initiatives, they can really create the perfect trifecta for sustainability.

How to Lead with Technology Tools

Knowledge is power! Time is currency! Spend your time gaining the knowledge you need to be successful.

Survival today means leaning on technology in order to reach consumers in the marketplace, especially the technology-driven younger generation.

Thanks to new technology, there are several ways for a company to provide customers with a better brand experience. A few examples of new disruptive technology platforms used to engage customers and win over their brand loyalty are:

1. **360-Degree Content** - 360-degree content is an interactive photo or a video recording shot in every direction.
2. **Digital Twin** - Digital Twin is a precise virtual model of a real-life object, process, or system. A digital twin is possible even if the physical object does not exist. They are great for displaying detailed data, monitoring data, and running and controlling simulations.

3. **Virtual Reality (VR)** - VR is a computer simulation. It immerses the user inside a virtual world, allowing them to interact with the environment. VR tries to stimulate as many senses as possible to make the user feel as though they are part of the virtual environment.

4. **Augmented Reality (AR)** - AR enhances the user's perception of the real world. It does that by adding a computer-simulated layer of information on top of the virtual environment. The most important benefit of AR is that it feels like a natural extension of reality.

5. **Mixed Reality (MR)** - MR brings together VR and AR into an enhanced version of AR. Sometimes it is even called augmented reality 2.0 because MR aims to achieve better immersion than AR alone. It integrates whole virtual objects into the real world. The technology responds to changes in the environment and user interaction in real-time.

6. **Pervasive Gaming** - Pervasive games are ones that take place in the real world often using elements of VR or MR.

Last but not least, companies rely on data and intelligence to make smarter and more substantive decisions which are where Big Data and AI come into play.

With Technology, a Virtual Experience Becomes Reality

Perception is reality and many have perfected the practice which forms the basis of our perception and experiential management business. Leaders use thought-provoking research to accent issues, needs, and concerns. We identify platforms, channels, and vehicles needed to communicate numerous advocacy agendas to drive a broader and more dynamic experience to the marketplace.

Successful leaders also craft high-powered experiential campaigns to drive more loyalty with the public and brand so companies can gain more influence and stature.

The perception only sets an expectation for people as they approach an event (virtual now) or branded experience. Once a visitor crosses the threshold into your space, the environment needs to meet or exceed those expectations by immersing them in an experience. It does not have to be a realistic experience or even a practical one, but it does need to evoke an emotional connection to your brand.

Be authentic, tell your story!

People have always been interested in the background stories behind products and services because they provide an opportunity to experience the product and company on a different level. Today taste, smell, and appearance are not enough to attract consumers. The product "story" gives the consumer an opportunity to experience the product on a different, more subtle level, which evokes a strong association with the brand.

Rather than looking at consumers as passive receivers of messages, we believe that consumers should be actively involved in the "production" and "co-creation" of marketing programs by helping develop a relationship with the brand through an experience. This can easily be accomplished by market intelligence surveys to garner the data and intel needed from consumers to help substantiate the need to fulfill consumers' needs and wants prior to buying.

By using the technology tools available today, industry leaders can provide the following plans and update older marketing programs to survive and sustain in downtimes. Technology combined with a tight PR plan can help generate more robust programs, such as:

Product Tie-Ins.

Whether the company is using the product itself or an explicit tie-in with the brand, any experience targeting prospective customers needs to weave in a selling aspect. It is not enough to simply entertain customers; they also need to be motivated in some way to investigate and purchase the product.

Loyalty Programs & Incentives.

It costs more to gain a new customer than it does to keep an existing one. Current customers will spend, on average, 67% more than new ones. No wonder customer loyalty programs are so hot! These programs reward customers for frequent and repeat purchases, often with special gifts or points. But the real payoff is that they are great for gathering important demographic information about your customers, which in turn allows you to tweak your marketing messages and strategies. For another twist on incentives, try including a free gift with each purchase made - loyal customers will remember the thoughtfulness of the effort.

Conducive to Building a Crowd.

Great experiences are shared, either by drawing a crowd to watch a movie or by creating an experience that is better when shared with others, which is where we lean on social media platforms to share and connect with others.

Listen to Feedback.

One thing is clear: Taking a proactive approach to collecting customer feedback ensures you never stray too far from the needs of your community, even as those needs evolve. Feedback is a powerful guide that provides insight and charts a path forward for every part of a company - from product through UX and customer support. This is especially important when it comes to customer satisfaction. Creative campaigns can get customers talking about products in unexpected ways, and if nothing else, you can learn what does and does not resonate with your audience in terms of keeping their interest. Market intelligence surveys are an ideal way to get the feedback you need from customers while staying on top of industry issues and trends.

Creativity Above All Else.

Things that capture people's imagination to the point where they simply must share it are key ingredients to a successful campaign. Companies have spent millions of dollars on failed tests simply because they thought money would bring attention to an otherwise boring, unoriginal angle.

According to Merriam-Webster, to thrive means "to grow or develop well or vigorously." Successful leaders thrive not just survive! They have the strength to stand up, rise-up, beat the odds, and lead in ways you never thought possible because they never give up on an idea, a goal, or a cause. Technology assists industry leaders to become sustainable, which is the key to success and innovation in the marketplace.

Be an Industry Leader

It is important to not lose sight of the 3W's:

- Who are you?
- What are you capable of?
- Where are you going?

These three questions will help to navigate and survive through uncertain times regardless of what chaos is swirling around you.

Who are you?

There are different types of leadership in business: Authoritative and Market. Authoritative leaders are the individuals whose voice is seen and heard when and where it's critical. They have respected voices and clear advocacy in their respective industries which we read about, see quoted in the news and on social feeds, etc. They use knowledge, intel, and experience to motivate and inspire others. We let them shape our perception.

Market leaders are the companies who are leading the market with their products or services. Their brand is the one that resonates with the trust and credibility impacting our purchasing decisions.

As a leader, the big question is are you an extension of your brand, or is the brand an extension of you? Leadership may come in all shapes and sizes, but true leaders all have the same underlying characteristics – ambition, drive, and a clear and defined mission. True leaders run their companies based on knowledge, definitiveness, and decisiveness. Most critical of all, they never run their companies based on ego. Ego is the #1 killer of start-ups.

What are you capable of?

Leading is not easy. Making easy decisions is not a test of true leadership, making hard decisions is the true test of character in a leader. Some say the grass is always greener on the other side. It is not greener, it's just a different shade of green. A successful leader needs to decide which side they can best grow and thrive in to support the business and help it to be sustainable.

Where are you going?

In order to get clarity on your industry's target market, you need to cut through the noise and clutter to gain a clear picture of your consumer. What raises the volume in your business life and makes it too hard to hear the next move for your brand? What clutters your inbox, newsfeed, or meeting schedule that is keeping you from performing at your best?

When it comes to noise – DIAL IT DOWN. This can come in the form of filters and resetting boundaries. The goal is to start pushing the brand forward and focusing on the path and not the clutter. The most effective leaders understand the 3W's and have applied technology to better execute their vision in the marketplace.

Cutting-edge technology offers an abundance of tools to facilitate these important leadership tasks. This allows for a stronger, more sustainable business that will weather future fluctuations in the marketplace. Be sure to lean on these technology resources to be successful in future endeavors.

CHAPTER 16

CYBERSECURITY – MOVING UP FROM THE KID'S TABLE

By **SHANNON WILKINSON**

Over the past several years, there has been a change in many business leader's mindsets from viewing cybersecurity as an "IT problem" to the idea that cybersecurity is an integral part of the overall business strategy. In other words, cybersecurity has moved from sitting at the kid's table to now being at the adult table, in this case meaning the Board of Directors.

If there is any doubt as to the potentially catastrophic impacts of a successful cyberattack, one only needs to look to Arkansas-based telemarketing firm The Heritage Company, which laid off over 300 employees and closed its doors just days before Christmas in 2019 after failing to recover from a ransomware attack that struck the company in October of that year. The company had expected to be able to restore access to its accounting and mail systems in just one week, but nearly two months later and even after paying the ransom, the company still had not been able to recover years of records, lost hundreds of thousands of dollars, and finally was forced to make the decision to close its operations.

With these types of stories and with the realization of the significant impact of cybersecurity in business strategy and operations, we have seen the rise of new positions within corporations to reflect the focus on cybersecurity and reduce business risk from cyberattacks. Companies now employ a variety of C-level positions from Chief Security Officer (CSO), Chief Information Security Officer (CISO), Chief Privacy Officer (CPO), and Chief Data Officer (CDO) to name a few of the newer titles working under the umbrella of cybersecurity and data privacy. These roles often report directly to the Chief Executive Officer (CEO), Chief Operating Officer (COO), Chief Financial Officer (CFO), and sometimes the Chief Information Officer (CIO).

These newly titled business leaders are providing input and visibility into business risks associated with cybersecurity events to executive leadership and corporate boards when before, this information would stop within the Information Technology (IT) department. Instead, information about the business risk associated with cybersecurity incidents or vulnerabilities affecting the organization can regularly be found in board presentations now.

One of the challenges that cybersecurity executives have when presenting to the board is translating the technical details into business operational risk and demonstrating a return on investment (ROI) for cybersecurity budgets. Calculating ROI within cybersecurity has been a challenge for many security executives, as the standard ROI formulas do not work well within the cybersecurity space. However, one effective method of measuring ROI that cybersecurity leaders have started to use is to look at the **expected loss (EL)** from a security incident **weighed against the cost of a project to reduce the organization's risk.**

For instance, let's say a company with no firewall had a successful ransomware attack launched against its corporate network and it took company operations offline for seven days. This resulted in a loss of X dollars of revenue each day, X dollars in employee overtime for recovery efforts, X dollars in outside consultants to help in the recovery/investigations, and X dollars for regulatory/litigation costs. Adding all these numbers gives an EL cost for the incident. But if the company purchases a firewall, the EL cost of the same incident would be reduced to four hours of lost revenue, no employee overtime, significantly lower costs for investigative consultants, and lower regulatory/litigation costs.

We can calculate the return on investment (ROI) for the purchase of a cybersecurity product using the EL before the product is implemented, subtracting the EL after the product is implemented, subtracting the cost of the product, and then dividing that all by the cost of the product. For instance, the new firewall costs $250,000. Prior to the purchase, the EL would cost the company $3.5 million. After the purchase, the EL would be $750,000.

ROI = (EL before purchase – EL after purchase – cost of the product) / cost of the product = ($3,500,000 - $750,000 - $250,000) / $250,000

Considering cybersecurity budgets, two things that have been points of contention and the subject of much debate within the cybersecurity community has been the reporting structure of cybersecurity to Information Technology leaders and the resulting competition for budget of IT versus cybersecurity. To many, having cybersecurity teams reporting into the IT department is much like asking your accountant to audit their own books. The thought is that very rarely would your accountant come back to you to tell you that they are doing a terrible job and you should fire them. Having the cybersecurity team report technology vulnerabilities into the IT department can result in the "brushing off" of problems that open an organization up to cyberattacks.

Additionally, having cybersecurity compete for budget against IT results in important cybersecurity projects that could significantly reduce an organization's risk being scraped, postponed, and canceled. Organizations should consider allowing the CISO, CSO, CDO, or CPO to report directly to the CEO, CFO, or legal department to ensure that cybersecurity risks are being properly addressed and the organization is making its best effort to secure itself.

In addition to seeing cybersecurity budgets discussed and risks disclosed at the board level, we are now seeing disclosures about the business impacts of cybersecurity incidents in corporate regulatory filings with organizations like the SEC. Prior to its July 2020 ransomware attack, wearables company Garmin noted in their December 2019 SEC filing that a cyberattack could have devastating consequences on the company as they collect, store, process, and use personal information like names, addresses, phone numbers, email, and payment information, in addition to wearable and customer health data such as height, weight, age, gender, heart rate, sleeping patterns, GPS location, and activity patterns.

Garmin has paid what is believed to be a $10 million ransom to gain access back to its systems after a week of their operations being affected because computer systems were taken offline by the ransomware attack. The longer effects of the ransomware attack and the reputational impacts remain to be seen as the events are continuing to unfold during the time of writing. However, with the speed of class action lawsuit filings following significant data breaches, there is no doubt that we will see a data breach settlement lawsuit filed in due time on behalf of Garmin's customers.

Since recognizing cybersecurity as an integral part of the executive C-level team, many organizations have moved from telling their technology teams from a "We have acquired a particular company, go take a look at their technology" approach to instead now engaging the technology teams, particularly cybersecurity, in the merger and acquisition (M&A) process and now saying, "We are thinking about acquiring this particular company, take a look at their security and tell me what business risks there are." By demonstrating the integration of cybersecurity in the M&A process, we can look to recent examples of how cybersecurity events have significantly impacted company valuations and the M&A process.

Perhaps one of the most notable examples is Verizon's acquisition of Yahoo in 2017. Originally, Verizon offered $4.83 billion in cash to Yahoo in July 2016. However, after news emerged in late 2016 that Yahoo had experienced several data breaches, including the theft of over one billion account credentials and a separate breach of the information of 500 million suspected to be carried out by a state-sponsored actor, Verizon reconsidered and shaved $350 million off the offering, and the companies agreed to a sale price of $4.48 billion in February 2017. In this example, Yahoo not only had to deal with the embarrassment of admitting significant cybersecurity events had occurred, but there was also a great deal of speculation that Verizon might withdraw their offer due to the magnitude of the attacks and the very public embarrassment of Yahoo's failure to detect and stop the data breaches. Nearly three years after the deal was finalized, the deadline for consumers to file for compensation just passed on July

20, 2020, as part of a $117.5 million data breach settlement stemming from the two data breaches.

Another recent example of a cybersecurity incident impacting an acquisition can be found in the three-way merger of DraftKings, SBTech, and Diamond Eagle Acquisition Corp (DEAC). Following the merger in April 2020, DraftKings filed an S-1 with the SEC disclosing that SBTech, an online gambling technology provider, had suffered a ransomware attack on March 27th, right before the merger was finalized, which resulted in SBTech shutting down its data center and suspending services for nearly one week. Noted as immaterial, customers were compensated for the downtime of the company's services, but DEAC renegotiated the merger and required SBTech to create a $30 million emergency fund to cover any future costs and litigation fees associated with the cyberattack.

Evaluating a potential target company's cybersecurity and data protection policies, procedures, and safeguards during the M&A due diligence process can significantly reduce the acquiring company's risk profile. It does so by surfacing shortcomings during the acquisition process and requiring the target company to remediate issues prior to the closing of the deal or gives the acquiring company the visibility and time to develop a plan for the remediation upon closing. Failure to discover vulnerabilities and remediate them before or immediately following an acquisition can result in significant reputational and litigation impacts for the acquiring company.

A notable example of failing to uncover cybersecurity vulnerabilities during the M&A due diligence process and remediate following the acquisition can be found in Marriott's 2016 purchase of the Starwood Group. In 2018, a security tool alerted Marriott of an attempt to access a guest database. During the investigation into the incident, Marriott discovered the intrusion dated back to 2014 under Starwood, the vulnerabilities were present during the M&A process, and that the breach had potentially compromised the information of 500 million guests of the corporation's hotels. Starwood Group, even two years after the acquisition, had still not been migrated to Marriott's reservations system.

Additionally, it was reported that Starwood Group security employees had difficulty securing their reservation system and the system had experienced a previous breach in 2015 that went undetected for eight months. Both of these issues should have raised red flags to Marriott in the due diligence process had they been thorough enough in their assessment of the cybersecurity of Starwood Group. Following the discovery of the breach, Marriott became responsible for the litigation costs and faced several class action lawsuits over the data breach which cite failures in the due diligence process, as well as criticize Marriott for failing to detect the breach sooner and waiting over a month to disclose the breach to affected customers.

While conducting the cybersecurity assessment for a target company, the acquirer may discover that the target has shortcomings in both technology and staffing. The acquirer should consider the costs of upgrading the cybersecurity technology of a target organization and adjust the offer based on those additional costs. For instance, if it will cost $1 million to purchase new cybersecurity technology and $500,000 in new staff salaries to cover staffing shortages, the acquiring company can consider reducing their offer by $1.5 million to cover the costs that they will incur following the purchase of the target. One of the last things that organizations want to do is thrust their cybersecurity teams into a situation where they do not have the budget to properly secure the organization or do not have the staff capabilities to cover the acquisition.

There is no doubt that the evolution of cybersecurity's role within the C-level and board will continue to change over time. As executives and board members now face professional and possible legal consequences of failures in cybersecurity strategy and protections, the cybersecurity leaders who once were seen as just being operational have been moved up from the kid's table to sit with the adults, contributing to the conversations on business strategy and risk. But it is important for executives and boards not only to allow cybersecurity to sit at the table, but they must also take warnings brought before them seriously and ensure that cybersecurity is given the budget it needs to properly secure the organization. Failing to do so could bring catastrophic consequences.

CHAPTER 17

SO WHAT, WHO CARES, AND WHY IT MATTERS

By **STEPHEN DEASON**

Men like to pee on things.

What in the world, you ask, do the urinal habits of men have to do with mission or leadership? It's simple. While men seemingly cannot resist peeing on things, what is shocking is their (our!) aim or our lack thereof. We apparently miss – a lot. In an attempt to reduce "spillage," the Amsterdam airport installed urinals with an etching of a fly inside the bowl. The idea – giving people something to aim for – decreased "spillage" by approximately 80%, resulting in direct cleaning savings of 8%. The question is: what would a near costless 80% improvement in behavior and an 8% improvement in your bottom line do for your business?

The fly is an example of a "nudge." This concept was brought into behavioral economics by Nobel Prize-winning economist, Richard Thaler of the University of Chicago, who calls the urinal fly his "favorite illustration" of a nudge. As described by Christopher Ingraham in an economic policy article in The Washington Post, "What's a urinal fly, and what does it have to with winning a Nobel Prize?" a nudge is a choice that "alters people's behavior in a predictable way without forbidding any options or significantly changing their economic incentives." In short, a nudge makes it easier – or more enjoyable – to do the right thing.

Nudges and their parent field of behavioral economics provide tremendous insights relative to both mission and leadership. Specifically, while humans often show rational behavior in large groups, on an individual level we often show limited rationality, strong social preferences, and reveal a significant lack of self-control. Hence, nudges matter, as do the mental shortcuts we use, our anecdotes and stereotypes, and our internal dialogs and narratives. In short, the framework we use to describe ourselves and our world is impactful. To a large degree, our aim in life depends on our framework, and when our framework is misaligned, results include a lot of "spillage."

Purpose-Driven

My (Our!) organization, The OPA RASA Group, is purpose-driven. Our purpose is to leverage capitalism to help people improve their aim – to reduce spillage in their lives. By doing so, we work to make the world a better place. We didn't get here on accident, and although that story begins nearly 40 years ago, a good place to start is with my first sales position. Because nothing happens until something gets sold.

"So what? Who cares?" were the questions ringing in my ears. I was a first-year salesperson. My boss was unhappy with my performance, and these were the questions that followed my radical failure to present well during my first sales job. I had failed to connect the dots for our prospects, and – to be fully transparent – I'd thrown up in a hall bathroom after dumping a cup of hot coffee into the lap of their CFO. It was a somewhat unpleasant day.

While that story ended well – I stood on stage later that same year and received an achievement plaque from the CEO – what has never left me is the importance of understanding the answers to those two simple questions: So what? Who cares? Said differently, why am I doing/saying/selling, and who is the person to whom it matters most? If I can answer those questions, then I'm on a mission, and *mission matters*.

Since then, over the last two and a half decades, I've struggled, learned, and applied those questions. So what, who cares? I've failed and I've succeeded. I've led, built, and turned around organizations and companies, picked up an MBA, an MSc, and am ABD in a Ph.D. program in business, adding a ton of graduate hours in business, economics, sociology, psychology, data science, and mathematics to my resume. I've also struggled with addressing and overcoming childhood trauma, drug and alcohol addiction, ignorance, and my past. I've stood on stage giving keynote addresses and receiving awards for business acumen; I've shared my story with thousands of people in the hope that at least one person in any given audience is helped in some small way. In short, I'm human. I've created spillage, and my job is very simple: be authentic, take responsibility, clean up my messes, and be of service.

Sell to Save Lives

I have a forthcoming book titled *Valued: How Purpose-Driven Businesses Can Conquer Addiction and Marginalization in America.* That book is all about being of service. Because good sales is good service, and – still – nothing happens until something gets sold.

Sales often gets a bad rap. When thinking of salespeople, we often envision a somewhat seedy person desperately attempting to take our money at any cost. And there's no doubt that those people exist, however, contrast this with a true salesperson - a person providing something of value. One who behaves like sports agent Jerry Maguire (played by Tom Cruise), interacting with Rod Tidwell (Cuba Gooding, Jr.), saying, "Help me help you." True salespeople are all about being of service, and we can all relate to and value that concept.

In *To Sell is Human*, Daniel Pink notes that we're all in sales. Most of us, in fact, are tremendously effective salespeople. We're generally most effective when what we're selling improves the lives of the people we sell to. Through sales, we can improve the lives of our families, friends, communities, countries, and the world. And that's exactly what social enterprise is about.

At the organization I serve and lead, every sale we make helps save lives. We are purpose-driven by definition. And that makes sales enjoyable for each of us. Simply put, sales is the ability to "move" others to engage in economic exchange. It's at the core of the "invisible hand" that helps supply and demand reach equilibrium in economic markets. Which is just a fancy way of saying that we exchange what you have for what I have at a price we agree upon. From time immemorial - long before Adam Smith's *The Wealth of Nations*, our sales skills have been crucial determinants of our survival and happiness. They remain so today. We are all in sales, all the time. So, the question isn't "Do we sell?" it's "How can we become better at selling?"

Let's start by recognizing that, contrary to popular belief, good salespeople are not born, they're made. Sure, some people have advantages - just as a taller person often has advantages on a basketball court. That said, according to work by Adam Grant, the most effective salespeople are ambiverts – people falling closer to the center of the introvert-extrovert scale. In other words, most of us.

The reason for this is that our effectiveness as salespeople – and as humans – is determined primarily by our ability to connect with one another. Whether "samurai," "solution," "spin," or any other consultative sales approach, our focus is on the other person, their wants and needs. Hence, connection is crucial, and that's an area where most of us already excel in at least some parts of our lives. But how do we do that better?

We find or create a mission. Mine is in helping people connect – connecting the dots, connecting with society, connecting with one another, with themselves, or with capitalism. Other people have other ways of creating a mission and creating connections. For example, in his NYT best-selling book and a TED talk with over 25 million views, Johann Hari teaches us that the opposite of addiction is connection. In my book Valued, I contend that connection not only has value, but I also go one step further in providing guidelines on how to find and cultivate that value.

Do Well and Do Good

Whether recovering from addiction, marginalization, or disenfranchisement, there is tremendous value in overcoming adversity. There is even greater value in creating social enterprises that are the embodiment of purpose-driven organizations. Social enterprises built to serve marginalized populations have wonderful advantages in the provision of goods and services in the pursuit of making the world a better place.

This concept is important for two primary reasons. First, because – often to our detriment – our society holds the attitude that doing well and doing good are separate and incompatible, despite evidence suggesting otherwise. In *Valued*, I address this concept by reviewing amazingly successful companies and reasons why they achieve above-average results. Second, consider the health impact of doing meaningful work, and of having a mission. Analysis of over 40 studies shows you won't die as young – there is a 22% decrease in mortality among people who perform meaningful (volunteer) work – while similarly, purpose-driven work appears to favorably impact life satisfaction, well-being, and decrease depression. So, it's simple – become mission- and purpose-driven and do what matters.

In addition to living a longer, more satisfied, and healthier life, there are two reasons to focus on your mission. The first is that you can spend the time of your life simultaneously doing things that create wealth while doing things that matter. It's been said, "You can't create time," but that's not true. Time is money and money is an output of the creation of wealth. Money is simply stored time. Hence, time can be created. And, like money, time can be wasted, spent, or invested. However, time and money are finite. We should maximize our use of both. Doing well while doing good maximizes over happiness, effectiveness, wealth, and time.

Second, on the topics of legacy and wealth creation: In April of 2015, Dave's Killer Bread sold to Flower's Food for $275 million in cash, showing once again that social enterprise models create outsized returns for both society and shareholders. To repeat, a bread company sold for over a quarter of a billion dollars! Proving once again the old adage, "Do what you love and money will follow." So, do work you love – work that matters – and the financial results will follow. I write on these topics, and we build businesses because we believe in simultaneously creating philanthropic and economic value – building a thoughtful legacy. Your legacy will exist; your choice is whether you create your legacy thoughtlessly or thoughtfully. If you want at least a modicum of control over your legacy, you must begin with the end in mind. You must first answer the question, "What do I value most?" Think deeply about what kind of person you want to be, and what you want your life to look like.

Social Enterprise and Capitalism

For me, that answer is social enterprise. Social entrepreneurship is both here to stay and a viable alternative to traditional business models – creating defensible business strategies while producing value for society and returns for shareholders. In *Valued*, I take readers on a journey through social enterprise models and their success factors. I ask readers to explore their passion, find their purpose, and start the process of simultaneously engaging both humanitarian and capitalistic instincts. I do this because my life is not my own, it is God's.

I begin with the greatest wealth-creation engine and the greatest social change agent: capitalism. As we consider the economic philosophy of capitalism, we enter a world where your ownership of companies, the "means of production," and the profit outputs of those companies are influenced by concepts such as private property, capital accumulation, wage labor, voluntary exchange, the price system, and competitive markets. This is our world – if you know how it operates, you have tremendous advantages. We started with sales, we now move to production, to management.

As you consider capitalism, consider management. Well-performing management has long been recognized as a fundamental force in business and in life. In his 1890 book *Principles of Economics,* Alfred Marshall wrote, "For the business by which a person earns his livelihood generally fills his thoughts during by far the greater part of those hours in which his mind is at its best; during them, his character is being formed by the way in which he uses his faculties in his work, by the thoughts and the feelings which it suggests, and by his relations to his associates in work, his employers or his employees." Performed well, management is the noblest of professions, paraphrasing the late Harvard Professor, Clayton Christensen. This is true because management has such a tremendous impact on the lives of those we manage. The impact of management on the mental, spiritual, and physical well-being of those being managed cannot be overstated.

How We Got Here: On History and Style

My management style, and that of the companies I serve and run, centers on creating environments of learning, openness, authenticity, vulnerability, attention to detail, and focusing on our mission. We are purpose-driven. None of this came about by accident. I am a person in long-term recovery, I'm a business executive, and I'm open about both. There are reasons, and I'll spend the next few paragraphs sharing a bit about why.

"My life is a gift, my job on this earth is to give it away," I said in closing as my story was broadcast to 55,000 people. I was on stage at Cox Enterprises in Atlanta, Georgia at the invitation of Judy Fitzgerald, the Georgia Commissioner over the Department of Behavioral Health and Developmental Disabilities. My role was the "designated survivor" as opposed to the "identified patient" during Cox's annual employee health conference. Joining me on stage was a cast of Emmy award-winning journalists, newscasters, physicians, and psychologists.

Born in Texas, I grew up on a farm in rural Alabama where I was exposed to some of the best and the worst of humanity. I escaped the physical, mental, emotional, and sexual abuse at 16 years old through a combination of luck and the Early College Admissions Program at UAB. Until 2015, my life was a series of severe complex PTSD-related recapitulations of my early experiences, combining wonderful leaps forward with awesome Icarus-like failures. Today, I use my story and the Phoenix-Icarus phenotypes of my story, life, and heritage to help others. Mixed metaphors aside, my family are virtually all addicts: alcohol, heroin, religion, or business – all in the sense of William James' *The Varieties of Religious Experience*.

"I had no hope, and I was sure my life was over, and then I heard your story, and now I have hope...because you are just SO F**KED UP!" gasped a tearful lady into my chest one Tuesday evening. I smile now because that encapsulates why I've experienced what I've experienced - why my "turning point" is where God placed it.

First, my background is sufficiently varied to be relatable and entertaining enough to make a good story. At least some of my experiences are relatable when I speak authentically from a place of vulnerability. Second, I am resilient, and resilience breeds hope in others. My trauma therapist says no one should have survived what I've survived. I share this so that others can experience hope. Third, because people mostly cannot injure me more than I've already been injured, the economic "cost" to me of vulnerability is relatively lower, perhaps, than that of other people. Hence, when I use my experiences to be of service to my fellow humans on this journey we call life, it's not bravery, it's pragmatism – and it works. The results have been amazing, and I work hard to help others find their path forward from wherever they are.

For instance, since realizing that my life is a gift from God and my job on this earth is to give it away in service, I've experienced tremendous internal and external success – in friendships, awards for innovation, leadership, keynote speaking, writing, and in building our social enterprise. I am deeply convicted that Service Mindsets are much superior to Greed or Survival Mindsets. Hence, our present and future industry are in social enterprise.

Purpose-driven capitalism is the greatest social change agent ever invented by mankind. We use this philosophy in our businesses. Our holding company, our operating companies, and our foundation are presently using and will continue to use capitalism to address inequality, marginalization, and the addiction challenges that face our country and our world. This is important because our world is struggling, and those struggles are accelerating.

Last year, in a keynote speech to 175 tech entrepreneurs and CEOs, I addressed the impact of machine learning on our idea of work. Society is moving into a period of intense and lasting change in both how we relate to one another and how we measure the value we bring as part of our daily lives. We are approaching a period of great opportunity, job creation, and social change. The Chinese symbol for crisis comes to mind, "wei" + "ji" represents "danger" and "opportunity." Yet the vast majority of humanity remains illiterate in the sense of Alvin Toffler: "The illiterate of the 21st century will not be those who cannot read and write, but those who cannot learn, unlearn and relearn."

Societal Values

"How can we help?"

Societally, we must redefine work, learning, connection, and value. For instance, we have learned that the opposite of addiction is connection, not sobriety. Recovery is a process, not a destination. Similarly, connection helps address inequality, marginalization, and disenfranchisement. In a society filled with pseudo-connections, we believe that building worth and creating value via the socially conscious use of capitalism can help address many of society's deepest challenges.

I do not merely "believe" this. Evidence suggests it works and works well. Over the last four years, I have worked often and deeply with addicts and other marginalized populations, bringing them into our businesses, teaching and demonstrating how using capitalistic philosophies can build worth and create traction in their lives. I have also developed and taught classes at numerous treatment and mental health centers. The results are amazing – in just four years, we have eleven "graduates" with more than two years in recovery, we've had zero relapses, and an average post-program wage of $75,000, an increase of 350%.

At OPA RASA, we are scaling our programs, looking to do more. Following my initial capital infusion, we have raised more funds and gained additional traction. Changing the world takes time, and genetics implies I have another three decades. And, this is where I plan on investing my second half of life. This is my Purpose and my Mission. I hope this has helped inspire you to elevate yours.

CHAPTER 18

ENGAGEMENT IS OUT; COHESION IS IN

By **DR. TROY HALL**

Engagement is one of the most commonly overused terms in current management circles. Of course, all employers want an engaged employee because they believe a "fully absorbed into the culture" type of employee will be more productive. And for a good reason, as 63 percent of all employees seek some sort of advancement. It's costly to replace organizational talent. Today's going rate to replace organizational intelligence is 25 percent of the employee's salary. That's on top of the expenses associated with recruiting, acquiring, and onboarding them, and then providing necessary training and orientation programs.

Numerous human resource publications and the general consulting world have lulled management to sleep with the "Engagement Lullaby." The song is filled with the rhetoric that organizational culture begins with filling the workspace with enthusiastic and empowered individuals. When in actuality, organizational culture should begin with cohesion - a workplace where people have a sense of belonging, are valued and agree to mutual commitments - before focusing on engagement. Employers are misguided to think that the primary method of achieving high levels of production and employee retention is to focus on the singularly faceted, cultural dimension of engagement.

Observation of Engagement is Inconclusive

Whether intentional or not, employers believe if they observe certain behaviors as engagement activities, they will become qualified to assess which employees are "all in" and committed. It's important for organizational leaders to understand that employees are not necessarily engaged just because they show up for work on time, complete tasks with little or no errors, are friendly to teammates, and don't seek a whole lot of direction. While those behaviors are well intended and portray a positive perspective, they do not conclusively mean the employee is positively and enthusiastically engaged. It merely means the employer has employees who come to work on time, do their jobs, and don't need a lot of direction from the boss.

Here's the problem with only relying on empirical evidence from an outward point of view: Observations not adequately measured and quantified may lead to a different set of conclusions than initially perceived. Just because employees give the leader "good vibes" that things are going well, doesn't mean it's an accurate reflection of what's actually happening across the company.

Satisfied and happy employees do not guarantee engagement; it signals contentment. Researchers have released findings that indicate employee satisfaction does not mean employees are "engaged" in their jobs, surroundings, or co-workers. Satisfaction, like engagement, is entirely unrecognizable when the employee intends to mislead others into believing things are fine. The truth of the matter is that employees can fake engagement.

The Cohesion Phenomenon

All is not lost. In a tongue-in-cheek way, saying "engagement is out; cohesion is in" is a theatrical way for me to set the stage for understanding the Cohesion Phenomenon. My Ph.D. research focused on group dynamics in the realm of global leadership and entrepreneurship. I studied organizational and social behavior to better understand how groups and individual talent perform, and how their performance can lead to engagement. Without bias, this research supported the hypothesis that cohesion positively impacts performance in all stages of a group's life cycle.

Through years of research and careful study, theorists have concluded that cohesion is a measurable, attainable phenomenon. Simply put, cohesion has a causal relationship to performance. When cohesion is present in an organization, it is causation, not correlation. Correlational outcomes in research are the measurement of two variables to understand and assess the statistical relationship between them with no influence from any extraneous variables.

One of the biggest fallacies in referring to research is using correlational inferences to predict behavior. To illustrate, let's take the correlation between rainy days and umbrellas. I can assert the correlation value between rainy days and opened umbrellas to be statistically high. However, one cannot say that a rainy day causes umbrellas to open. On a rainy day, there is a strong correlation that due to the weather, more umbrellas would be open. But the rain alone did not cause the umbrella to open. People can open umbrellas for other reasons, such as testing them or opening them to shade themselves from the sun. Also, individuals can shelter themselves from the rain without opening umbrellas, such as putting a newspaper over their heads or wearing rain gear.

A causal relation between two events occurs if one causes the other. The first is called the event and the second is called the effect.

My research supported that cohesion, the main event, causes performance, the effect. Cohesion's outcome is predictable, not accidental. The result of cohesion is performance, and performance, in turn, leads to engagement. This is the Cohesion Phenomenon.

Cohesion = Performance = Engagement

Leaders within global organizations of all sizes and industries recognize the value of functional groups to accomplish a series of activities aimed at achieving a shared purpose or task. This cohesion between team members is essential for an organization to reach its performance apex. The added value of building cohesion into the work culture is that productivity increases and employees are engaged.

Cohesion Culture™

I do not disagree that employers want employees who are engaged. Understanding and applying the Cohesion Phenomenon explains why leaders should be more intently focused on creating cohesive environments and work teams. When leaders shortchange the process by trying to leapfrog over performance, they establish an unpredictable foundation built upon engagement, where employees lose and companies falter. Today's global leaders are creating Cohesion Cultures™ because they understand that cohesion occurs in all cultures, work environments, and throughout generations. Cohesion is a multi-cultural event.

In my bestselling book, *Cohesion Culture: Proven Principles to Retain Your Top Talent,* I teach the three elements of cohesion: 1) a sense of belonging, 2) value of people, and 3) mutual commitment.

All three elements - belonging, value, and mutual commitment - are needed to guarantee cohesion is present.

People are naturally drawn to belong, to become part of some-thing special. It's in our DNA to connect with other people. Theorists such as Maslow's Hierarchy of Needs, Hoggs' Social Identity Theory, and Klein's, Bion's, and Freud's research on relationships support this fact; humans have an innate need to connect. A remarkable thing happens once people commit to a group. They give part of their identity to the group and will do extraordinary actions to keep the group together and to ensure its success.

Do not underestimate a person's need for intrinsic motivation. Once the desire to belong has been satisfied, an individual seeks to understand their value, know their purpose, and be recognized for their contributions. When these pieces come together, they fuel a person's desire to achieve. Talent that feels valued is 87 percent less likely to leave an organization. Being able to spot the warning signs of a dysfunctional culture, then get ahead of the issues, positions leaders to act accordingly. Leaders have the opportunity to establish a mindset that fosters cohesion through actions of shared feelings, including a team atmosphere that offers appreciation when employ-ees perform value-added work. This is very important to bring the employee-employer relationship closer together.

Finally, the coup de grâce of cohesion is the mutual commitment between the employees and the organization. Creating a high-per-forming and enthusiastic relationship between talent and business is exactly what leaders want when they seek employee engagement. When people see that the organizational leaders focus on the needs of the people first - versus corporate goals - the drive toward a compatible commitment is set into motion. When management is only focused on employer commitment, the relationship becomes one-sided. The employee feels like an object. This leads to the talent feeling disconnected and unappreciated. The solution to fixing this one-sided relationship is the leader aligning employee development and personal goals with corporate objectives and outcomes. This entirely mutual commitment bridges the gap of the desired, harmonious relationship between employee and employer.

A work culture created through cohesion is continuously in motion and always evolving. The impact of leadership upon the work environment cannot be understated, denied, or overlooked. Supplying employees with access to learning, opportunities for collaboration and advancement, and engagement in social connectivity supports the framework of a healthy workplace. A Cohesion Culture™ is more than just words to describe a work environment. It is the foundation on which leaders build an organizational strategy and corporate synergy aimed to keep talent engaged now and into the future.

Four Aspects of HR Strategies that Support a Cohesion Culture™

Cultures built upon the framework of cohesion incorporate four aspects of employee needs into their human resource strategies and practices. They include intellectual stimuli, emotional or spiritual growth, physical and mental well-being, and financial mindset. Collectively, these aspects support cohesion and its elements of belonging, value, and mutual commitment.

Intellectual Stimuli

Talent stays where they feel they belong, are developed, and are frequently challenged intellectually. A key characteristic of today's workforce is the display of an entrepreneurial spirit. Employees desire autonomy and a collaborative work environment where they are asked to think critically and are encouraged to contribute. The company is investing in the growth and intellectual well-being of an employee by supporting team building, an open exchange of ideas, and signaling to this talent pool "you belong here, there is a place for you."

Emotional or Spiritual Growth

More than ever, people want to understand their purpose. Many people seek a connection with the universe, a higher power, or themselves to support the belief that they matter and that what they do makes a difference. Organizations want to sound off about employees having passion. Yet, it's not until senior leadership aligns an employee's purpose with the organization's mission that their passion becomes more than window dressing. Passion is the emotional feeling a person experiences when they are doing what they know is important and has value.

Physical and Mental Well-Being

Organizations often neglect taking full advantage that a healthy employee is a productive one. Peak performance is impossible without attention to well-being, a key driver of mutual commitment. When employees are healthy or have the support to sustain a wellness mentality, they are more satisfied and exhibit behaviors consistent with cohesion. Part of a robust human resource strategy and processes mindset is having the systems in place to support more than simple performance evaluations.

Financial Mindset

Claiming financial independence and security is another import-ant aspect of mutual commitment. Educating employees about money management has a powerful and positive impact which extends to the employee's personal life. Keeping an employee financially fit lessens the mental burdens of financial stress so they can perform at a higher level. When an organization creates conver-sations that promote individual financial wellness, the organization supports a mindset that encourages financial stability. Teaching financial awareness and understanding in the areas of savings mobi-lization and credit utilization can help individuals toward achieving independent financial success.

Top Three Ways to Ensure the Success of a Cohesion Culture™

Cohesion Culture™ is a people-centric focus that starts with core values. Once this value system is identified and defined, it must inte-grate with every aspect of the organization's fundamental human resource strategies and practices. The dynamics of creating a culture of cohesion include the integration of values, beliefs, attitudes, and behaviors. There are three simple ways leaders can ensure the suc-cess of their culture to bring about performance and the ultimate prize of engagement.

Cultural values are based on honesty. Organizational values must be sourced from the truth and reflect the organization's characteristics if they have any meaning at all. This value system sets the expectation of how employees within the organization interact with each other and with those outside the company's four walls. Values are the foun-dation for employee behavior. For the most part, typical dysfunctions within an organization occur when people do not operate with honesty and authenticity as a core value. If the culture does not reflect the truth of what management says and does, employees will know it. And when the leadership is not authentic in representing itself to the talent, then their top talent will begin to seek employment elsewhere.

Without exception, the culture starts with the Chief Executive Officer and the senior leadership team. If the company's senior-most leaders do not display the organization's values, the culture will become fragmented, fractured, and will fail. It's not hard to recognize that when the company's leadership teams do not support the core values, guiding principles, or value statements, the organization will suffer. Additionally, the senior leadership team must support the four aspects of intellectual stimuli, emotional growth, employee well-being, and financial independence. In other words, the gap between "what the leader says" and "what the leader does" must be negligible, or the culture suffers.

Live it, breathe it, and own it. Fundamentally, "living it" means people observe, imitate, and adopt the actions of leaders who demonstrate effective leadership attributes. These seven attributes include being teachable, showing compassion, extending grace, demonstrating humility, seeking the truth, having pure intentions, and making peace. "Breathing it" refers to how employees accept these cultural behaviors and values to integrate them into how they perform with and for others. "Owning it" is the employee taking accountability and responsibility to uphold the organization's value structure as if they were a member of the senior leadership team.

Putting It All Together

It's not your grandpa's world anymore. Gone are the days where employees feel an overall sense of achievement by merely holding down a job. Today's workforce wants to express themselves through an entrepreneurial spirit, collaborative teamwork, purpose and meaning, and social connectivity. Senior leadership can no longer expect employees to wait patiently on the sidelines for advancement opportunities, or to find nobility through performance alone.

Make no mistake: cohesive teams are productive. Both employees and the company benefit from the increased performance and a productive employee-employer relationship. Organizational leaders' efforts to create and sustain Cohesion Cultures™ will have a significant positive impact on teamwork, performance, and talent retention, and in the end, attaining engagement becomes less ambiguous and more planned.

CONCLUSION

By **ADAM TORRES**

Business leaders come from many backgrounds. Their stories are infinitely varied. Along the way, they experience success and failure. Some of the leaders presented are further along their leadership path than others, but one common trait is shared among all of them. They are never done working on their craft. They continue to push forward to test the boundaries of what they think they are capable of. Above all, this one trait will be responsible for much of the innovation that occurs in our generation and the generations that follow. Leadership is fundamental to our future success, not only in business but in our society at large.

To your success,

Adam Torres

P.S. Don't forget to listen to our podcasts at **MissionMatters.com**

APPENDIX

Adam Torres | Introduction | Page iii
Co-Founder Mission Matters
MissionMatters.com
Instagram: @AskAdamTorres
Twitter: @AskAdamTorres

Alejandro Badia, MD, FACS | Chapter 1 | Page 1
Hand & Upper Extremity Surgeon at Badia Hand to Shoulder Center
www.drbadia.com
Founder, CMO, and CEO at OrthoNOW Immediate Orthopedic Care Centers, LLC
www.orthonowcare.com
Co-Founder of Miami Anatomical Research Center
www.MARC.institute
IG: @drborthonow
FB: @badiahandtoshouldercenter
LinkedIn: https://www.linkedin.com/in/drbadia/

Ashu Bhatia | Chapter 2 | Page 11
VP - Digital Strategy and Transformation
Daugherty Business Solutions
AshuBhatia1@yahoo.com
Twitter: @ashuATL
LinkedIn: https://www.linkedin.com/in/ashubhatia/

Brian Patrick | Chapter 3 | Page 23
Founder/CEO of GREENLIGHT Inc. / The Platinum 2000 Group, Inc.
brp@greenlightstartup.com
Facebook: @P2KGroup
Facebook: @Greenlightstartup
Instagram: @RatedGenX
Twitter: @Brpatrick1
Twitter: @Greenlightstart
Twitter: @P2KGroup
LinkedIn: https://www.linkedin.com/in/brianpmp/

Bruce Elfenbein, | Chapter 4 | Page 33
Certified Financial Fiduciary®
CEO of SecuRetirement, Inc.
bruce@secureretirement.lfe
Facebook: Bruce Elfenbein; SecuRetirement, Inc.; The Good King
Twitter: @belfenbein
Instagram: securetirement_inc
LinkedIn: https://www.linkedin.com/in/bruceelfenbein
www.securetirement.life
www.nodebtandhappy.com

Chris Reavis | Chapter 5 | Page 43
Founder, Avid Intent
chris@avidintent.com
Web: https://avidintent.com
LinkedIn: https://www.linkedin.com/company/avidintent
Facebook: @avidintent
Twitter: @avidintent

K. Eric Aguilar | Chapter 6 | Page 55
CEO of Omnitron Sensors
Board of Directors at Ascent Robotics
LinkedIn: https://www.linkedin.com/in/eric-aguilar/
Twitter: @OmnitronSensors

Gregory Shepard | Chapter 7 | Page 65
CEO & Co-Founder, BOSS Capital Partners
https://www.bosscapitalpartners.com/
https://www.gregoryshepard.com/
LinkedIn: https://www.linkedin.com/in/gregshepard/
Facebook: https://www.facebook.com/greg.shepard.77
Twitter: https://twitter.com/GregShepard_
Instagram: https://www.instagram.com/gregshepard_/

J.C. Granger | Chapter 8 | Page 75
CEO of Infinity Marketing Group
Website: www.InfinityMgroup.com
Email: JC@InfinityMgroup.com
LinkedIn: https://www.linkedin.com/in/jcgranger/
Twitter: @jcgranger

Dr. Joseph C. McGinley, M.D., Ph.D. | Chapter 9 | Page 87
mcginley@mcginleyinnovations.com
mcginley@mcginleyclinic.com
CEO | Founder - McGinley Orthopedics
www.intellisensedrill.com
Founder | Physician - The McGinley Clinic
www.themcginleyclinic.com
CEO | President - McGinley Manufacturing
www.mcginleymanufacturing.com
Founder | Course Director of McGinley Education
www.mcginleyinnovations.com
Facebook: @McginleyInnovations
Instagram: @mcginleyortho
Twitter: @McGinleyOrtho
LinkedIn: McGinley Orthopedics
YouTube: McGinley Orthopedics

Kurt W. Snyder | Chapter 10 | Page 99
President, The Colby Group of Companies
ksnyder@colbydirect.com
www.colbybpo.com
www.colbydirect.com
www.colbyinsuretech.com
LinkedIn: https://www.linkedin.com/in/kurt-w-snyder/
Twitter: @ColbyDirect1

Martin Rowinski | Chapter 11 | Page 111
CEO of boardsi
Boardsi.com
martinrowinski.com
LinkedIn: https://www.linkedin.com/in/martinrowinski/
Facebook: @martin.rowinski
Instagram: @martinrowinski
Twitter: @rowinskimartin
boardsi Social Media:
LinkedIn: https://www.linkedin.com/company/boardsi/
Facebook: @Official.boardsi
Twitter: @boardsi2

La'Shion Robinson | Chapter 12 | Page 121
Founder & CEO at HUDLMusic
Twitter: @HUDLMusic
Twitter: @L_HUDLMusic
IG: @HUDLMusic
IG: @L_HUDLMusic
FB:@HUDLMusic
LinkedIn: Lashion Robinson

Michael Ralby | Chapter 13 | Page 131
Founder of Ralby Enterprises Inc.
ralby@ralbyenterprisesinc.com
Linkedin: https://www.linkedin.com/in/michaelralby/
Twitter: @michael Ralby
Instagram: mbralby
Facebook: Michael Ralby

Robert R. Wolf | Chapter 14 | Page 143
President of Terra Firma Business & Financial Consultants, LLC
Asset Coach & Tax Strategist
robert@assetcoachtaxstrategist.com
rwolf@terrafirmaconsultantsllc.com
LinkedIn: www.linkedin.com/in/assetcoachtaxstrategist
Facebook: @asstecoachtaxstrategist

Sarah Miller | Chapter 15 | Page 153
CEO, Axis Entertainment, Inc
Founder & CEO, Media Excellence Awards
smiller@axis-entertainment.com
www.Axis-entertainment.com
Facebook: https://www.facebook.com/AxisPublicRelations/
IG: @axisentertainmentofficial
www.mediaxawards.com
Twitter: Mediaxawards
Facebook: https://www.facebook.com/mediaxawards/
LinkedIn: https://www.linkedin.com/in/sarahmillerla/
IG: @GlamourgirlLA
Facebook: https://www.facebook.com/GlamourGirlLA
Twitter: @GlamourgirlLA

Shannon Wilkinson | Chapter 16 | Page 163
CEO, Tego Cyber Inc
https://tegocyber.com
info@tegocyber.com
Facebook: @tegocyber
Twitter: @tegocyber
LinkedIn: https://www.linkedin.com/company/tegocyber
Twitter: @SWilkinsonCyber
LinkedIn: https://www.linkedin.com/in/swilkinsoncyber/

Stephen Deason | Chapter 17 | Page 171
CEO of The OPA RASA Group, LLC
Executive Chairman of The OPA RASA Foundation
stephen@oparasa.com
LinkedIn: https://www.linkedin.com/in/stephendeason/
Facebook: @StephenEDeason
Instagram: thestephendeason
https://www.oparasa.com
https://www.oparasa.org
https://www.opastaffing.com
https://www.opamedstaffing.com
https://www.opatechstaffing.com

Troy Hall, Ph.D. | Chapter 18 | Page 183

Author | Global Expert on Talent Retention | Speaker | Consultant

DrTroyHall@gmail.com

www.DrTroyHall.com

LinkedIn: https://www.linkedin.com/in/drtroyhall/

Facebook: @DrTroyHall

Twitter: @DrTroyHall

Instagram: @DrTroyHall

Listen to our
PODCASTS

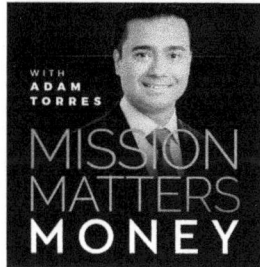

MISSION MATTERS
WE AMPLIFY STORIES

www.MissionMatters.com

The
PODCAST MATTERS
SCHOOL

Why Did I Start This School?

Every day, I interview business owners, entrepreneurs, and executives. I've done over 1,500 podcast episodes.

Depending on when you read this, I'll likely be over 2,000 episodes!

Many of the people I interview ask me to help them launch their own podcast. My ultimate goal is to help people spread their story and message. So, of course, I started helping people one by one. I figured that the more people I can help start podcasts, the more people I would help spread their message. Mission accomplished.

But then things got a little out of control. See, I have a habit of over-committing. It got to the point where helping people launch their own podcast was taking up more time than I had available.

So, I was faced with two choices.

One, I could tell people that I just don't have the time to help them.

Or, two, create a podcast school for those who want to launch a podcast or continue to grow their reach for an existing podcast.

I wanted to continue helping people, so the school was born.

What Makes This School Different?

First, this course is NOT designed for people looking for a way to make a quick buck.

The course is designed for busy professionals who have always wanted to start a podcast but have never had the time or knowledge to get one started. Others who will benefit from the teachings in this course are the part-time podcasters who can't quite figure out how to grow their audience.

While I'm not claiming that I've seen all podcast courses ever made, I can tell you that when I was first getting started, it seemed like all of the courses were really long and felt like part-time jobs just to complete. Well, I wasn't looking for a part-time job, I had a business already and I just wanted to podcast.

So, my commitment to you is that each lesson in this course will be straight to the point. Most videos are under five minutes and many of them are two minutes or less. Why? Because you don't need to hear me drone on. You just need the information so you can take action. Less time learning and more time in action is what will grow your podcast.

Finally, though it's kind of weird for me to say this considering I had almost 14 years of wealth management experience before going full-time into media about three years ago, but this is what I do for a living.

This is not a "side hustle" for me. I get paid to podcast, not just to teach. Why do I tell you this? Because you want to learn from someone who lives and breathes what they are teaching. You don't want someone experimenting with YOUR time.

For more information visit **MissionMatters.com**.

Happy Podcasting!

Adam Torrey

OTHER AVAILABLE TITLES

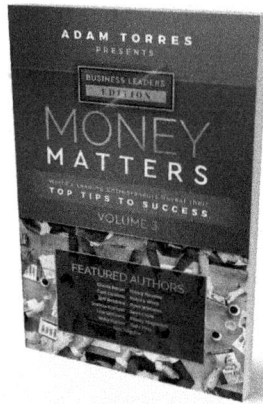

In the third edition of *Money Matters (Business Leaders Edition Vol 3)*, Adam Torres features 13 top professionals who share their lessons on leadership. In these pages, through inspiring stories, you'll discover:

- Different approaches to leadership and people management.
- Rules for success from a Green Beret.
- How to effectively manage a company full of millennial employees.
- How to transform your marketing mindset.
- Where customer success and employee success meet.
- What manifesting your success in business looks like.
- And much more.

Purchase at **MissionMatters.com**.

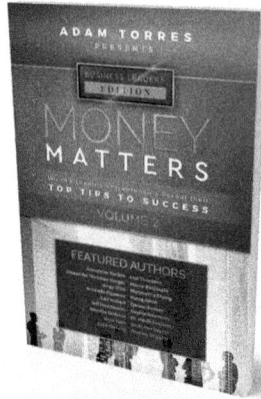

In the second edition of *Money Matters (Business Leaders Edition Vol 2)*, Adam Torres features 18 top professionals who share their lessons on leadership. In these pages, through inspiring stories, you'll discover:

- How to harness the entrepreneurial mindset.
- Why scaling your business for sustainable growth is vital.
- How to grow your eCommerce business.
- Lessons learned from sales experts.
- How to level up your leadership.
- How to manage your energy.
- And much more.

Purchase at **MissionMatters.com**.

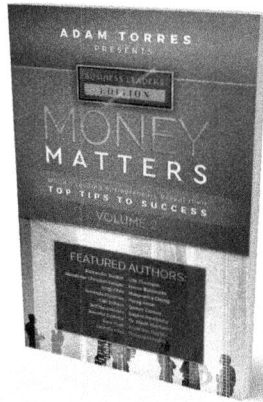

Navigating the world of real estate can be stressful. Are you getting closer or further away from your goals?

Adam Torres is here to help you move forward. In his latest edition of *Money Matters (Real Estate Edition Volume 2)*, Torres features 13 top professionals who share their lessons in real estate.

In these pages, through inspiring stories, you'll discover:
- How to get more properties through syndication.
- How to implement servant leadership to have a more successful business.
- Why investing in real estate is not just for rich people.
- How important insurance is in real estate transactions and what to look for.
- Why using a private lender can help you in real estate transactions.
- What legal options you have to protect your assets.
- And much more!

Purchase at **MissionMatters.com**.

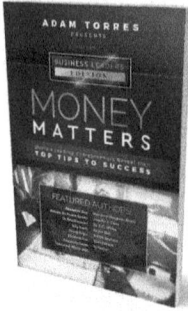

In the original edition of *Money Matters (Business Leaders Edition)*, Adam Torres features 15 top professionals who share their lessons on leadership. In these pages, through inspiring stories, you'll discover:

- How to create a clear path for growth.
- Why every business should act like a media company.
- How to build a community to last a lifetime.
- Lessons learned from professional soccer.
- How to maintain a well-connected brain for peak performance.
- How to create harmony through union in business.
- And much more.

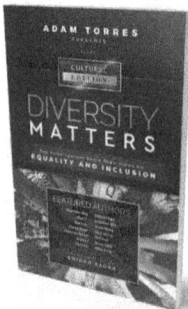

Embracing diversity and inclusion in a rapidly changing business landscape can be challenging. Are you and your organization positioned properly for this new age of connectivity? Torres features fourteen top Asian leaders who share their lessons on diversity, equality and inclusion.

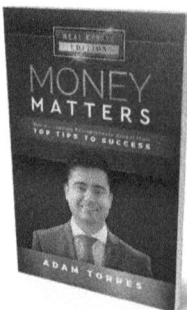

Navigating the world of real estate can be stressful. Are you getting closer or further from your goals? Finance guru Adam Torres is here to help you move forward. His guide, Money Matters, features 15 top professionals who share lessons from their more than 250 years of combined experience.

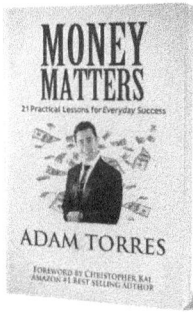

In this clear, concise manual, financial expert Adam Torres goes over the basics of personal finance and investing and shows you how to grow your wealth. Torres makes sure you are prepared for whatever life throws your way. It's never too early to think about the future and his book will give you the right tools to tackle it.

All books available for purchase at **MissionMatters.com**.

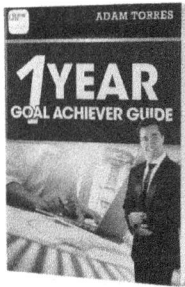

This workbook has been designed specifically for individuals like you who are dedicated to improving the results in all areas of your life. By following the ideas and exercises presented to you in this transformational workbook, you can move yourself into the realm of top achievers worldwide.

Download for free at **MissionMatters.com**

www.ingramcontent.com/pod-product-compliance
Lightning Source LLC
Chambersburg PA
CBHW060548200326
41521CB00007B/525